Vietnam
Cambodia
Laos

SAY IT

ENGLISH	VIETNAMESE
Good morning, good day	*Xin chao*
How are you?	*Ong* (man)/*ba* (woman) *co khoe khong*
Well, thank you	*Toi khoe, cam on*
Goodbye	*Tam biet*
Yes	*Co, Vang*
No	*Khong*
What is your name?	*Ong* (man)/*ba* (woman) *ten gi?*
My name is...	*Ten toi la...*
I do not understand	*Toi khong hieu*
Please	*Xin ong* (man)/*xin ba* (woman)
Thank you (very much)	*Cam on (rat nhieu)*
Excuse me...	*Xin loi anh*
Help!	*Cuu voi*
I want to get to... /where is?	*Toi muon di...*
...hotel	*...khach san*
...bank	*...nha bang*
...post office	*...buu dien*
...market	*...cho chanh*
...hospital	*...benh vien*
How much?	*Cai nay gia bao nhieu?*
I need a doctor	*Toi can mot bac si*
Where are the toilets?	*Phong rua mat?*
Today	*Hom nay*
Tomorrow	*Ngay mai*
Aeroplane	*May bay*
Boat	*Thuyen may*
Bus	*Xe buyt*
Bicycle	*Xe dap*
Motorcycle	*Xe moto*
Mosquito net	*Man, mung*
Drinking water	*Nuoc suoi*

KHMER	LAOTIAN
Chum riap	Sabaidee
Niak sohk sabai de?	Sabaidee bo?
Knom sohk sabaiq	Sabaidee, kop chai
Li ahs	La koon
Baat (man),/Ja (woman)	Tyao/Euh
Tay	Bo
Niak chmuah ei?	Jao seu nyang
Knom cmaah...	Koy sou...
Tee knom min yaal tee	Koy bo kao chai
Soum	Kaloona
Ar koun	Kop chai
Suomto	Ko tot
Juay knom phwang	Suay dae!
Phleuv naa teuv...	... you sai?
Santakea	Hong hem...
Thniakia	Thanakaan...
Bprai sa nee	Paisani...
Psaa	Talaat...
Monti paed	Hong mo...
Ponman?	Tao dai?
Juay hav krou paet mao	Koy tong kan ha mo
Bongkohn neuv ai naa?	Hong suam you sai?
Thngay nih	Meu ni
Thngay saik	Meu eun
Yaun hawh	Hua bin
Duuk	Hua
Lan thom	Lot may
Gang	Lot thip
Moto	Lot chak
Mung	Mung
Toek	Nam doom

CONTENTS

1	Vietnam
81	Cambodia
129	Laos

Fold-out maps
- I The Mekong
- II Cambodia, Phnom Penh, Angkor
- III Laos, Luang Prabang, Vientiane

VIETNAM

**Bernard Joliat
and
Sonia Vian**

JPMGUIDES

ancient traditions

CONTENTS

3	**This Way Vietnam**
7	**Flashback**
17	**On the Scene**
17	The North
31	The Centre
49	The South
65	**Shopping**
67	**Dining Out**
69	**Sport and Entertainment**
70	**The Hard Facts**
80	**Index**

Features
55 The Mighty Mekong

Maps
59 Sa Dec
75 Hanoi
76 Hué
77 Ho Chi Minh City Centre (Saigon)
78 My Tho
79 Vinh Long

Fold-out map
The Mekong

a natural elegance · A fascinating culture · steeped in legend

THIS WAY VIETNAM

Content to have shaken off colonialism and the deprivations of hardline socialism, Vietnam has taken significant steps towards a market economy by opening its frontiers to tourism, trade and investment. Though it was weakened by the long and painful war of independence, the average standard of life is constantly improving, poverty is diminishing and the cheerful faces that welcome visitors bear witness to a new-found optimism.

A lesson in geography

The Vietnamese say that the map of their country resembles the bamboo pole with huge baskets balanced at each end that they use to carry goods to market. One basket represents the Red River delta, the other the Mekong delta.

Bordered on the north by China, on the west by Laos and Cambodia, and open to the Gulf of Tonkin and Nam Hai (South China Sea) on the east, Vietnam covers a land area of 332,378 sq km (128,332 sq miles)—almost as large as Germany. This long, narrow strip of land, in places no more than 50 km (31 miles) wide, has a dense population of over 88 million. Vietnam is divided into three geographical regions. The capital, Hanoi, with more than 3 million inhabitants, lies in Tonkin, the northernmost region, at the heart of the fertile delta of the Red River. The mountainous terrain of the centre, Annam, is dominated by the port of Danang and the ancient imperial capital of Hué (population 340,000). The wide delta of the Mekong in the southern third of the country (Cochinchina) embraces Ho Chi Minh City—still known by its old name, Saigon—today Vietnam's most populous city with more than 7 million inhabitants.

The Vietnamese people (Kinh), who live mostly in the plains and the urban centres, make up the country's largest ethnic group (86 per cent of the population), with 54 cultural minorities scattered along the border regions.

Mountains and plateaux cover three-quarters of the country. The rest is lowlands, forming a green patchwork quilt of fields and paddies stitched together by rivers and canals. Offshore are thousands of islands. The highest peak is the 3,143-m Fan Si Pan (or Hoang Lien Son) in the north.

The Essentials

Careful planning will enable you to see in a fortnight the best of the countryside and a fair share of the cultural attractions of this amazing country. A first visit ought to include most of the essential sites of the cities and the coast—Hanoi, Ha Long Bay, Hué, Danang, Hoi An, Nha Trang, Dalat, Ho Chi Minh City and the Mekong delta—with perhaps an excursion to meet some of the varied ethnic groups who live in the mountainous border regions.

Ho Chi Minh City

Life in the former Saigon is lighthearted, buzzing along at the same speed as its millions of motorbikes and increasing number of cars. In contrast to the street life of China, the atmosphere here is carefree, chaotic and exuberant. Unless you are filled with nostalgia for colonial days, it will not be the stately buildings lining the streets of Saigon that leave the most lasting impressions, but rather the frenetic lifestyle of the people.

Stall-holders are now doing more business than ever, cleverly salvaging and recycling anything that comes their way, creating desirable goods out of items you would probably have thrown into the bin without a second thought.

Two hours from Ho Chi Minh City, the small city of My Tho is reached by way of a scenic road bordered by paddy fields, fruit trees and orchids. Bathed in an indefinable light, the city is linked to the immense Mekong delta by various waterways. From each of the cities on the nine channels of this great river, boats transport their passengers to floating markets or tropical gardens, and into scenes straight out of the film *The Lover*, inspired by Marguerite Duras's novel which was partly based on her own life.

Northeast of Ho Chi Minh City, in pleasant hill country, the town of Dalat, at an altitude of 1,475 m, offers a different aspect of Vietnam. In this refreshing wooded region, dotted with lakes and waterfalls, the daily market is the meeting place of the various ethnic minorities.

The Centre

Nha Trang and its neighbouring islands form a beautiful coastal resort, the ideal place to relax after a journey along the Mandarin Road. Opportunities for water sports are wide-ranging here, and the area will delight everyone interested in ancient cultures.

Danang, in the centre of the country, has an excellent museum devoted to the Cham culture, good preparation for an excursion to My Son, the capital and intellectual and religious centre of the ancient kingdom of Champa. In nearby Hoi An, surrounded by rice paddies, UNESCO has listed almost 850 buildings which are of importance to Vietnam's cultural heritage.

North of Danang, in the imperial city of Hué, you'll encounter some of Vietnam's most beautiful historic sites, legacies of the long line of Nguyen rulers. Situated on the Perfume River, Hué (once known as Phu Xuan) mingles the romance of its serene landscapes with the splendour of a bevy of palaces, pavilions and tombs.

Hanoi and Ha Long Bay

In Hanoi, the Mot Cot (One Pillar) Pagoda and the Temple of Literature (Van Mieu) go back almost a thousand years. There are dozens of pagodas in the city and the surrounding area. But Vietnam's past can also be explored in the Museum of History, the Museum of the Revolution and the Museum of the Army, which have become places of pilgrimage for France's Indochina combatants and American Vietnam War veterans, as well as the Vietnamese themselves. And you don't need to be a veteran to feel the atmosphere at the many battlefield sites, where so many lives were lost.

From Hanoi, you can explore Ha Long Bay, where junks and sampans navigate their way skilfully around a dreamland of 3,000 tropical islets and limestone reefs, a natural landscape that has been described as the eighth wonder of the world.

Having seen all this, you will surely want to make a second trip, to soak up the timeless atmosphere that's present in every aspect of the country, from the savoury cuisine, the arts, landscapes and festivals, down to the very fragrances wafting in the air. Vietnam touches every heart.

A bay of legend. The 3,000 islets of **Ha Long Bay** surge high up from the waters, forming a bizarre aquatic labyrinth of craggy rocks in astounding sugar-loaf shapes. According to legend, the gigantic sculptures were created by a dragon who threw himself into the sea from his lofty lair, creating a network of fissures in the rocks below. When the sea rolled back after the cataclysm, it submerged all but the highest parts, which now compose a breathtaking wonderland. It has been listed by UNESCO since 1994.

Covered bridge built in 1776 at Thanh Toan near Hué.

FLASHBACK

The Vietnamese people (Kinh), the largest ethnic group in the country, claim to be the children of Au Co, who sat on a hundred eggs and hatched as many giants. The eldest of these, in 2879 BC, supposedly inaugurated the mythical dynasty of the Hung, whose 18 kings ruled over Van Lang, a kingdom in the Red River delta, until 257 BC.

The arrival of bronze with Indonesian immigrants at the end of the second millenium BC contributed to the rise of the Dong Son culture that was already established at this crossroads of Annam (central Vietnam) and Yunnan (south China). This first dynasty evolved to assimilate the influences of its Indonesian forebearers with Mongoloid strains from incursions of Viet and Tai peoples. From the 4th century BC, the marshland of the Red River delta was turned into an expanse of paddy fields, thus encouraging development.

Under the Thuc dynasty, (257–207 BC), the future Vietnam called itself Au Lac. Under Trieu rule (207–111 BC), it was known as Nam Viet and controlled much of southern China, but the situation was reversed when the powerful Han rulers of China conquered the region.

Chinese Domination

Under the Han dynasty, the country was known as Giao-Chi until AD 203. The story of the famous "Trung sisters' revolt" (AD 39–43) has been handed down over the ages. The sisters, widows of local aristocrats, led an uprising against Chinese rule. The revolt was briefly successful, and the older sister, Trung Trac, set herself up as ruler of an independent state. But a Chinese counter-offensive ended in the defeat of the Vietnamese—and the suicide of the Trung sisters.

Chinese domination of the Red River delta continued until the 10th century. Although the Vietnamese were never reconciled to Chinese rule, Confucianism and Taoism won over the population, and the medical knowledge of the Buddhists compensated for the tyranny of the administration. In 678 the inexorable expansion of

Vietnam began when the Chinese annexed a region south of Tonkin, naming it Annam, "Dominion of the South".

The Hindu Kingdoms

From the 1st century, the south of today's Vietnam belonged to the Hindu kingdom of Funan (or Phu Nam), which participated in the lively exchange of trade and artistic and religious traditions between East and West. Contacts were wide-ranging—a Roman medallion of gold struck in AD 152 and bearing a likeness of the Roman Emperor Antoninus Pius has been found at Oc-Eo, Funan's chief port in the western part of the Mekong delta. In the 6th century, Funan proved unable to resist the attacks of the pre-Angkorian kingdom of Chen La, and was annexed to this powerful Cambodian empire.

During the same period, another Hindu kingdom, that of Champa, occupied the centre of the country (the region of Danang as its heartland) from the end of the 2nd century. This kingdom gradually expanded south as far as Phan Rang, confirming its power by building grandiose temples and palaces.

The First Vietnamese State

In 938, the Vietnamese commander Ngo Quyen took advantage of the collapse of the T'ang dynasty to push the Chinese back to the north. The battle of Bach Dang River ended 1,000 years of Chinese occupation and won independence for Vietnam. The reign of the Ngo dynasty was short-lived, however, as at the death of Ngo Quyen (965), General Dinh Bo Lynh seized power. His Dinh successor was in turn dethroned by Le Hoan, who proclaimed himself emperor under the name of Le Dai Hanh. His dynasty is called the Earlier Le.

The succeeding Ly dynasty (1009–1225), founded by Ly Thai To, consolidated the kingdom of Dai Viet. In this period the first Vietnamese university, the Temple of Literature in Hanoi, was inaugurated. Meanwhile, the Chinese were still smarting over their defeat and launched several attacks against Vietnam, but each time they were repulsed by the strategy of Ly Thuong Kiet (1030–1105). This national hero also had to contend with vigorous offensives from the south by the Cham and the Khmer. In the end, the Vietnamese won the day, conquering and pillaging the north of Champa.

In 1225, the Ly dynasty was overthrown by the Tran who improved the irrigation of the Red River delta. Remarkably, they also repelled the Mongols who had conquered China as well as most of the rest of Asia.

Tonkin's Robin Hood

Ho Qui Ly usurped the throne from the Tran in 1400, only to see the Ming Chinese reappear in an explosion of extortion and brutality against the local people in 1406. A rich landowner, Le Loi, founded a centre of resistance in the village of Lam Son (Thanh Hoa Province) and fought the Chinese on behalf of the poor. He was a fair-minded man and prohibited pillage, thus becoming a much-admired local hero. The Chinese wanted to take advantage of his popularity and make him a mandarin, but this "Robin Hood of Tonkin" refused the honour, crushing the Chinese troops in 1427 and the following year proclaiming himself Emperor of the Dynasty of the Later Le, under the name of Le Thai To. That date marks the true birth of Vietnam, which, liberated from

Four interesting Cham sites. The ancient Hindu kingdom of Champa once occupied the centre of Vietnam, a region which has inherited some traces of this civilization. Its four most beautiful sites are to be found in the jungle of **My Son**, its spiritual capital; at the sanctuary of **Po Nagar**, on a hill overlooking Nha Trang; near Phan Rang-Thap Cham on the Dalat road at the summit of the Cham Acropolis of **Po Klong Garai**; and further south on another hill at **Po Rome**. The finest sculptures discovered at these sites are on display at the Cham Museum in Danang.

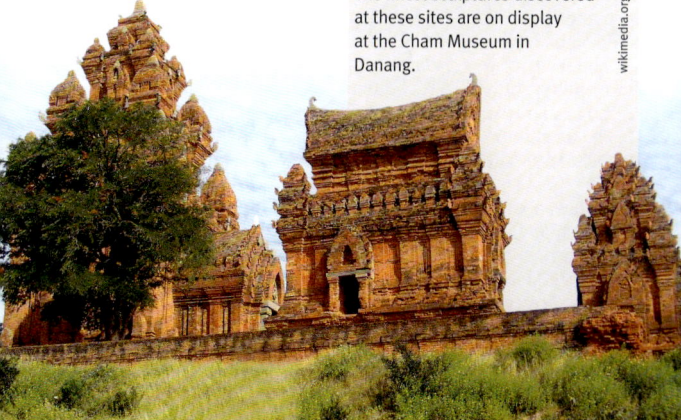

A Cham monument at Po Klong Garai, built in the Tham Mam style at the end of the 13th century.

Chinese cultural domination, went on to forge its own national identity and impose its rule on other territories. The last Cham soon became the victims of the Nam Tien, the "Great March South" commanded by emperor Le Than Ton. Their capital, Vijaya (Binh Dinh) fell to the Vietnamese in 1471.

The dynasty of the Later Le maintained its vigour until 1524, but continued to reign nominally until 1778. In fact, real power was shared by the Trinh family in the north and the Nguyen in the south, who effectively ran the country between them.

The First Europeans

The first Europeans to set foot on Vietnamese soil were Portuguese sailors, who disembarked at Danang in 1516. The Nguyen lords used the weapons brought by the foreigners, invading the Mekong delta and defeating the Khmer. By the 17th century, Cambodia was finally obliged to recognize the sovereignty of Vietnam.

The Portuguese had come to do business. They established a trading post at Faifo (Hoi An) with the Japanese and the Chinese, while the Dutch installed themselves in the north. Missionaries flocked in from all over. The credit for inventing *quoc ngu*, the phonetic adaptation of the Roman alphabet to the Vietnamese language, used today by the Vietnamese, belongs chiefly to the French Jesuit priest Alexandre de Rhodes (1591–1660). Imposed by the French during the 1950's, it remains Vietnam's official written language.

Most European merchants left the country towards the end of the 17th century, but the missionaries put down roots in Vietnam: the erudition displayed by the Jesuits seduced the imperial court.

The Nguyen Dynasty

In 1771, three Tay-Son brothers from the south revolted against their rulers, pitting their forces first against the Nguyen and then the Trinh. By 1773 the Tay-Son held the centre of the country, and within fifteen years their dynasty had replaced that of the Le. Saigon and the Mekong delta fell into their hands in 1783.

After taking refuge in Siam, 15-year-old Prince Nguyen Anh, the sole survivor of the fallen houses, reconquered the Mekong delta. With the financial support of a French bishop and French military advisers, he captured the Tay-Son stronghold in 1800 and the town of Hué in 1801. The following year, in Hué, the prince took the name of Gia Long and became emperor of the unified country, which he called Vietnam. He was the first of 13 Nguyen monarchs, a dynasty that ended only in 1945 when Bao Dai abdicated after the defeat of Japan and the success of the Vietminh. Throughout their long reign, from 1802 to 1945, the Nguyen emperors supported the development and unity of the nation.

Gia Long himself established citadels, dikes and lines of communication, notably the Mandarin Road between Saigon and China. But he advised his successor, Minh Mang (1820–40), to be wary of Westerners. A fervent supporter of Confucian culture, the new emperor rejected "barbarian" influences. Eventually, rebellions broke out all over the country and it closed its doors to foreigners. But they were not to give in without a struggle.

French Colonization

British victory in the first "opium war" in 1842 opened Chinese markets to their ships, but the emperors in Hué did not take much notice and continued their actions against foreigners, executing missionaries and murdering Vietnamese Catholics. This gave other Europeans a pretext for intrusion, and in August 1858 a fleet of 14 French and Spanish ships captured Danang. Saigon fell a short time later, and colonial forces took possession of the three provinces of Cochin China. In 1862 Emperor Tu Duc was forced to sign a treaty acknowledging this conquest, thus guaranteeing foreign vessels access to his ports and granting missionaries free rein.

French presence spread to the centre and north of the country, and in 1883 Tonkin became a French protectorate, followed by Annam a year later. The Union of Indochina was created in 1887, uniting Cochin China, Tonkin, Annam and Cambodia, and, six years later, Laos. However, the triumph of the Chinese republicans under Sun Yatsen in 1911, and the defeat of Russia by the Japanese, did much to encourage the nationalist sentiments of the Vietnamese. French rule became more repressive; all natural resources were exploited, with ever more plantations being developed. Cities expanded, transport networks improved and the population grew, but education was neglected.

The Republic

Nguyen That Thanh, the son of a mandarin born in 1892, visited London and the USA as a young man and lived in France from 1918, where he was a founder member of the Communist Party. This was Ho Chi Minh. In 1925 he assembled followers in the Thanh-nien, the embryonic Vietnamese Communist Party. Violent revolts marked the early 1930s. In 1941, Ho Chi Minh's

The traditional *ao dai* consists of a long tunic slit down both sides.

disciples founded the Vietnamese Independence League, with the Vietminh, who were to spread terror among foreign military forces, as its members.

The Japanese invaded Vietnam in 1940 but left the Vichy régime to govern for a while before deciding to take over themselves in March 1945. However, Japan's ambitions were swept away in August when atomic bombs were dropped on Hiroshima and Nagasaki. Ho Chi Minh seized the moment; his August Revolution gave him control over the north and the centre of the country. In September 1945, he proclaimed the independence of the Democratic Republic of Vietnam.

The Fall of Dien Bien Phu

After World War II, France wanted to re-establish colonial rule in the south, while Chinese Nationalist forces moved into the north. France negotiated the departure of the Chinese and then, in March 1946, signed agreements which confirmed Vietnam's independence, recognized by China and the Soviet Union. Some French troops were to stay, with a phased withdrawal, and a referendum in the south.

During the eight-year War of Indochina that followed, at least 36,000 French soldiers and around 175,000 Vietnamese soldiers were killed, without counting the thousands of civilians. In May 1954, after nearly two months of heroic defence, 10,000 exhausted French soldiers surrendered at Dien Bien Phu to Vietnamese forces led by General Vo Nguyen Giap, while most of northern Vietnam and Laos fell into the hands of the Vietminh. The following day, the Geneva Conference began, and eight weeks later the war in Indochina was ended.

The Conference provided that Vietnam be divided in two at the Ben Hai River, near the 17th parallel. The territory north of this line of demarcation became the (communist) Democratic Republic of Vietnam led by President Ho Chi Minh. Free movement of people between north and south was guaranteed for 300 days. Almost a million refugees, most of them Catholic, fled the north and settled in South Vietnam, under the leadership of Ngo Dinh Diem, who declared himself President of the Republic of South Vietnam following a sham referendum. The United States closed the American consulate in Hanoi.

The Vietnam War

In 1960, Vietminh supporters in the South formed the National Liberation Front (NLF)—disparagingly called the Vietcong—and launched effective guerila attacks against the Diem regime. The North decreed general mobilization, demanding reunification of the country and withdrawal of all military forces. With progressive infiltration by the army of the North (the NVA), coming along the "Ho Chi Minh Trail" through Laos to support the Vietcong raids, South Vietnam found itself in danger of collapse. Fearing a spread to other non-communist nations of the region (the "domino" effect), the Americans intervened and sent in advisors and military aid from 1961. They provoked the overthrow of Ngo Dinh Diem on November 1, 1963. A succession of coups was to follow, eventually bringing Nguyen Van Thieu to power in 1967.

Meanwhile, the war had escalated. The first American combat troops landed at Danang in March 1965; by the end of the year they numbered 185,000. Two years later, there were more than half a million Americans and 800,000 troops from South Vietnam, Australia, the Philippines and South Korea. Bombing raids were launched against North Vietnam, and vast areas of the South were sprayed from the air with highly toxic defoliants in a bid to deprive the Vietcong and NVA of cover. The side-effects are still in evidence today as people continue to be diagnosed with related illnesses.

The US Pulls Out

In early 1968, the US base at Khe Sanh was attacked by NVA forces. The Tet Offensive went on to shake the entire American nation. On January 30, a hundred Vietcong commando raids were launched Southern towns including Saigon, where the American ambassador narrowly escaped an attack on his embassy. After ten days of desperate fighting the communists were repulsed, but the psychological victory had given them encouragement. It also awakened the American conscience and international public opinion, traumatized by this pointless conflict. The newly elected President Nixon promised to work for peace and slowly reduced US troop numbers, but intensified the bombardment. Ho Chi Minh died in 1969.

The peace talks that had begun in Paris in 1968 finally ended in an agreement in January 1973. The United States withdrew all its forces, leaving behind a gigantic store of military hardware for its allies in the South. But once again, agreements were not respected: President Nguyen Van Thieu broke the cease-fire.

In January 1975, the North Vietnamese army crossed the 17th parallel and entered Saigon on April 30, nine days after the flight of Thieu. The Americans evacuated their embassy in total disarray. The two Vietnams were finally unified in July 1976 as the Socialist Republic of Vietnam.

Isolation

In 30 years of conflict, the country lost 3 million people, while 5 million more were mutilated. The socialist government rebuilt the economy and strengthened its hold through strict, hard-line socialism. This led to political, religious and intellectual repression in the South, where offenders were sent to "re-education" camps. From 1978, almost a million refugees fled Vietnam, mainly by sea in anything that would float, no matter how flimsy, some even using sheets as sails. According to the United Nations High Commission for Refugees, between 200,000 and 400,000 of these "boat people" perished at sea after facing storms, diseases and starvation; the survivors settled in the USA, Canada, Europe and Australia.

Backed by China, Pol Pot's Khmer Rouge attacked Vietnam in 1977. Strongly supported by the Soviet Union, the Vietnamese retaliated, took Cambodia and overthrew Pol Pot. The United States then imposed an embargo on Vietnam. In its turn, on the pretext of teaching Vietnam a lesson, China invaded some northern provinces in February 1979, but was pushed out.

A farmer's life in the ricefields in the region of Ha Long.

Opening Up

The withdrawal of Vietnamese forces from Cambodia after 1989 opened an era of détente in relations with the West and China. The Peace Treaty signed in October 1990 in Paris consolidated this. The withdrawal of the Russians from Vietnam in the 1990s accelerated reform. The defection of its communist "allies" encouraged Vietnam to adopt a policy of popular capitalism assimilated into a socialist state. The lifting of the American embargo in February 1994 permitted diplomatic and commercial relations between the two countries to resume. In 1995 Vietnam joined ASEAN, the Association of South-East Asian Nations. It joined the World Trade Organization in 2007.

Today, visitors are welcome and former refugees return to see family or to make investments. The tourist industry has benefitted hugely from these changes.

On the shores of Hoan Kiem lake, the perfect place to read or just contemplate the scenery.

ON THE SCENE

Abounding in natural and cultural wonders, Vietnam generously rewards travellers in search of authenticity. Comfortable hotels in line with Western standards have popped up all over the country, both in towns and at the historic sites. From the Chinese frontier to the Mekong delta, you are free to travel anywhere you please. But in a country ravaged by 30 years of war, much of the road network is still in poor condition, despite major schemes for improvement. The main attractions are easy to reach, but if you want to see places off the beaten track, often more gratifying, you should be prepared to invest a little more time and money.

The North

Hanoi

By setting up his capital in Thang Long, the City of the Soaring Dragon—today's Hanoi—Emperor Ly Thai To provided the independent kingdom of Dai Viet (Vietnam) with an ideal cultural site at the heart of Red River delta. Among Hanoi's three hundred buildings of interest, two of the most famous monuments date from Ly Thai To's era—the One Pillar Pagoda (Chua Mot Cot), and the Temple of Literature (Van Mieu). But first, look around the Old Town and the lakes, and save some time for the museums.

Ho Hoan Kiem

Most of Hanoi's sanctuaries are built around a legend. The story associated with the Lake of the Restored Sword, in the heart of the city, goes back to the 15th century when the Chinese occupied the country. A golden turtle living in the lake gave to one Le Loi, a local fisherman, a sword which he used to put the invaders to flight. Le Loi was made emperor and returned the sword to the turtle.

Den Ngoc Son (Temple of the Jade Mountain) stands on an islet near the north shore of the lake and is reached by crossing over the delicate little Bridge of the Rising Sun (The Huc).

Close to Hoan Kiem lake is Hanoi's **Water Puppet Theatre**; a performance of this delightful art form should not be missed.

Old Town
Nestling between the citadel and Hoan Kiem lake, the old town of Hanoi is a picturesque compendium of colonial architecture, ancient communal houses *(dinh)*, Chinese shops and workshops, pagodas and hidden temples. Indulge in the charming atmosphere, the lively and colourful street scenes and some unusual shopping. In this area you'll also find some of the most sophisticated restaurants in Hanoi, serving a range of Vietnamese and Asian specialities.

Many of the lanes *(pho)* have retained the names of the traders' guilds that were located here, or of the merchandise which was traded: Rice Street, Silk Street, Cloth Street, Paper Street, Oil Street, and so on.

The Imperial Citadel
The ancient imperial city of Thang Long, built in the 6th century and UNESCO listed, bears witness to all the historical changes which have occurred in the capital throughout the ages. The elegant 9th century stone dragons leading to the Kinh Thien Palace, the impressive north gate and the Flag Tower, symbol of Hanoi (1812), have all survived the ravages of time and war. The site has thousands of historically valuable archeological artefacts.

Vietnam Military History Museum
Situated to the south of the citadel, this museum's exhibitions relate the country's numerous struggles for independence, in particular the battle of Dien Bien Phu. The courtyard is filled with aeroplanes, tanks and artillery.

Van Mieu
In 1070, emperor Ly Thanh Tong dedicated a Temple of Literature to Confucius. Six years later it became the first university in Vietnam, a centre for Confucian philosophy and morality, originally reserved for the sons of mandarins and nobles.

The building was modelled along the lines of the temple of Qufu, the birthplace of Confucius, in China. An astonishing succession of doors, courtyards, pavilions and sanctuaries fill a walled enclosure 350 m in length and 60–75 m wide. The inscription at the entrance requests visitors to dismount before entering.

The central doors and aisles were reserved for the emperor, the side aisles for the mandarins and the military.

The Pavilion of the Khué Van Constellation opens onto the third courtyard, whose delightful architectural details are reflected in the Thieu Quang Tinh (Well of Celestial Light). Around the square basin, 82 stone turtles bearing stelae (originally there were 117) date from 1484 to 1779. What, you may wonder, do the inscriptions record? The answer: exam results—names of the successful candidates for coveted positions in the imperial civil service.

In the fourth courtyard, the sanctuaries were destroyed in 1946, but two traditional temples remain, dedicated to the cult of Confucius.

Chua Mot Cot

According to legend, Ly Thai To longed for a male heir. After a dream in which the goddess Quan Am offered him a small boy, he hastened to marry a pretty country girl, who soon gave birth to a son. As a symbol of his gratitude, he had the curious One Pillar Pagoda built in 1049. Entirely made of wood, it survived undamaged for almost 1,000 years, only to be destroyed by the French when they abandoned the city in 1954. Restored, but with a concrete pillar replacing the original wooden one, the lotus-shaped pagoda emerges from the middle of a lotus pond.

Mausoleum of Ho Chi Minh

Opened in 1975, the mausoleum stands north of Chua Mot Cot in Badinh Square, where the Independent Republic of Vietnam was declared in 1945. The embalmed body of the father of Vietnamese independence lies in a glass coffin in the air-condi-

---

Two unusual temples. At Tay Ninh, northwest of Ho Chi Minh City, the **Holy See of the Caodaists** is a shining example of religious eclecticism. Deriving its spiritual basis from the major religions of the world, Caodaism accepts almost all other faiths and embraces the great prophets along with celebrities from the world of the arts, literature, politics and learning. The **Temple of Literature** in Hanoi, dedicated to the cult of Confucius, is of great historic interest, and is also the scene of water puppet shows.

Alice Delvaille

tioned hall, contrary to his wish to be cremated. Lines of visitors, including foreign dignitaries, pay their respects at the mausoleum every day. Just next to it is a wooden house on stilts, which Ho Chi Minh had built for himself.

A short walk further north is the **Presidential Palace**, former residence of the French Governor General of Indochina, which Ho spurned for a more austere lifestyle. Walking around this area you will see some of the most luxurious villas of the colonial era.

More lakes

North of the citadel is **Ho Truc Bach** (Lake of the White Lotus). At its southwest corner, the Den Quan Thanh (Spirit of the North Pagoda) was erected during the Ly dynasty (1009–1225) and embellished in the 17th century by the addition of a beautiful bell and a 4 m high bronze statue representing the Spirit.

Just across Duong Thanh Nien, **Ho Tay**, or West Lake, is an old branch of the Red River. On a little peninsula stands the 6th-

---

Water puppets. Water puppet shows—Mua Roi Nuoc—are specific to the Red River region. Dating from the 11th century, they had almost become a forgotten art. When the tourist industry started to develop, the people took stock of their culture and saved this unique entertainment from oblivion.

The actors are painted wooden puppets that move about on a pool, accompanied by an orchestra playing in the background, in full view of the audience. The puppeteers, hidden behind a curtain or a bamboo screen, stand waist-deep in water to manipulate their tiny subjects, which represent villagers and their farm animals, kings, warriors and mythical beasts such as the phoenix, dragon and unicorn. Each satirical drama comprises several tableaux inspired by important topics such as great battles against the invader, the exploits of former kings, ancient legends, as well as the more mundane events of daily life. Singing, music and exploding fireworks underline the critical points of these enchanting fables. The Hanoi theatre's repertoire is exceptionally varied.

istockphoto.com/Furtado

century Tran Quoc Pagoda. It has an interior courtyard and a garden containing monastic funerary monuments.

History and Revolution Museums

Southeast of the old town, between Hoan Kiem lake and the Red River, you will see many European-style buildings, including the National Library and the Municipal Theatre, built in 1919 and resembling the Paris Opera House.

The National **Museum of Vietnamese History** covers all periods from neolithic times to the French colonial era, and has fine archaeological exhibits. The dominant theme, however, is the millennia-long struggle against the Chinese.

Just one block north of the History Museum, in a handsome French colonial building, the **Vietnam Museum of Revolution** documents the struggles of the Vietnamese from the arrival of the French in 1858 through to the end of the 20th century. Displays are divided into three sections with more than 40,000 exhibits.

Hoa Lo Prison

The French-built Maison Centrale, intended to hold Vietnamese political prisoners, was later used to incarcerate US prisoners of war in such dreadful conditions that it became known ironically as the "Hanoi Hilton". It was demolished in the 1990s but part has been preserved as a museum, including the interrogation room—with no sign of the acts of torture that were carried out there. It is several blocks west of the Historical Museum.

Den Hai Ba Trung

Among Hanoi's many sanctuaries, the Temple of the Trung Sisters, a 20-minute walk south of Hoan Kiem lake, illustrates the exploits of these two heroines. In the year 40, they bravely drove away the Chinese invaders and were crowned as queens. Three years later, they threw themselves into the river to escape the enemy who had returned in force. An engraved stele recounts their struggle.

Hanoi Museum

In the Tu Liem district west of the centre, this museum documenting the city's history, culture and architecture opened in 2010 as part of the millennial celebrations and has around 50,000 artefacts on display. Within its own park, the German-designed building is a spectacular inverted glass pyramid, the floors linked by a vast spiral ramp.

Vietnam Ethnology Museum

Some 7 km to the west of the city centre, this museum should not be missed. It was inaugurated in

1997 with the aid of the Musée de l'Homme in Paris, and retraces the customs and traditions, and the daily life, of the 54 ethnic groups living in the country. The exhibition is composed of objects, photographs and films and is divided into nine sections organized by geographic and linguistic criteria. Outside you can see several traditional houses, each one with its own specific furniture, and surrounded by vegetation typical of its region.

Excursions from Hanoi

Within a radius of 100 to 150 km (60–95 miles) from Hanoi, some of Vietnam's most beautiful natural and cultural sites are worth exploring. You will discover forgotten historic cities and villages inhabited by ethnic minorities of great charm. These trips will take you into the breathtaking limestone mountains, where any number of pagodas house welcoming Buddhist communities amid the paddy fields or in caves.

All of these places are accessible in a day trip from Hanoi, provided you set out at sunrise. An added benefit to starting out in the cool of the morning is that on the way you can watch people going about their daily work: villagers leading their ducks to ponds covered in lotus flowers; fishermen casting their wide nets into the canals; water-buffalo hauling rickety carts through the serene landscape.

Chua Huong

The Perfume Pagoda, a Buddhist place of pilgrimage in the mountains, lies 60 km (37 miles) south of Hanoi in the heart of Ha Tay Province. You could make the trip in one day, but even three days are barely sufficient to do justice to this site. Chua Huong is an enormous complex of sanctuaries dotted throughout the forests of a limestone mountain chain.

The road goes as far as the village of Ben Duc, beyond which the journey proceeds by flat-bottomed sampan. This is a magical hour of gliding silently along a labyrinth of canals, encountering the canoes of market gardeners, and floating past mysterious temples. The site itself has a network of steep mountain footpaths linking the twelve principal sanctuaries of the Perfume Pagoda, for the most part built in the 17th century on the mountainside or inside deep caves.

These sacred places, forming two groups of five and seven pagodas respectively, offer wonderful opportunities to the rambler. It would take several days to visit every one of these sanctuaries, an exercise reserved for passionate enthusiasts of Buddhist art. Most people are happy to settle for the glorious ascent up the irregularly paved path to Chua Huong Tich, the most interesting of the sacred caves at the summit of Huong Tich, the mountain of the Perfumed Imprint. There is also a cable car.

Near the landing-stage, there are two temples packed with enough statues and ancient objects to bring consolation to anyone who feels unable to tackle the long climb up to Chua Huong Tich.

Chua Thay

Dozens of other interesting pagodas are scattered over the countryside surrounding Hanoi. To the west, 40 km (25 miles) from Hanoi, Chua Thay (Pagoda of the Master) in Sai Son village is dedicated to Sakyamuni (Tich Ca) and his 18 *arhats*, or disciples. The villagers also refer to it as Thien Phuc, the Pagoda of Celestial Felicity. The statue of Master Tu Dao Hanh, a talented 12th century water puppeteer, stands next to the statue of his reincarnation, King Ly ThanhTong.

Chua Tay Phuong

The ironwood Pagoda of the West, 10 km (6 miles) from Chua Thay, boasts particularly attractive roofs and 74 statues of *arhats* dating from the 18th century and carved in jack-tree wood.

Chua But Thap

In Ha Bac Province, 30 km (19 miles) northeast of Hanoi, the Pagoda of the Paintbrush, surrounded by a stone gallery, is among the most handsome in Vietnam. It was built in the 12th century but has been remodelled several times since then, acquir-

---

Red River. Song Hong, the Red River, has its source in China near Dali, the ancient city of Yunnan. Vietnam's lifeline, 1,149 km (714 miles) long, is one of five fingers of water in the peninsula that constitutes South-East Asia. The other four are, from east to west, the Mekong, the Chao Phraya (or Menam), the Salween and the Ayeyarwady. The Red River's waters link the ethnic minorities of the mountainous "blue lands" to the wide plains of the pagoda-dotted "brown lands". Vietnamese identity was forged in its delta, where the precious silt fertilizes paddy fields and provides clay for the temple bricks—providing nourishment for body and soul. The idyllic landscape and smiling people of the delta region radiate a perfect serenity, but under the surface roils all the faith and powerful will of Vietnam. It is not easy to harness this versatile river, whose headwaters are so jealously guarded by China, but the Song Hong, despite its devastating floods, is the true catalyst of Vietnamese unity.

ing its unusual four-storey octagonal stone *stupa* in the 17th century. Note the ornamental pond carved from rock, next to a delightful stone bridge.

Inside the principal sanctuary, surrounded by a gallery of carved stones, a wooden statue of the goddess of mercy, Quan Am, she of "a thousand arms and a thousand eyes" is depicted. There are many other statues, as well as a functioning 13th-century carved wooden prayer-wheel.

Hoa Binh

At the foot of the mountains 80 km (50 miles) southwest of Hanoi, the town of Hoa Binh makes a convenient centre for visiting some of the varied ethnic groups who live in the area: Hmong, Tai, Dao and Muong. The Da river which flows through the town has been dammed just a short distance upstream, creating a reservoir 160 km (100 miles) long. Excursion craft make day trips to tribal villages dotted along its shores.

Tam Coc and Hoa Lu

Some 100 km (60 miles) south of Hanoi is the region of Tam Coc (Three Caves). With its paddy fields and softly rounded limestone mountains, it resembles the River Li in China, between Guilin and Yangshuo. Boat trips take you into the heart of this nat-

Lovely landscapes. The region of rice paddies and limestone promontories near **Tam Coc** composes a superb backdrop similar to that of Ha Long Bay; it is equalled only by the fields and mountains around Ben Duc, along the canals leading to the **Perfume Pagoda**. But Vietnam is a kaleidoscope of magnificent landscapes, such as the seascapes of the Hué coast at **Nha Trang**, the light of the **Mekong delta** near Can Tho, and the **terraced hillsides** of the mountain-dwelling ethnic minorities.

Huber/Morandi

ural paradise, where beautiful grottoes shelter a further profusion of temples of great historic and religious significance.

Hoa Lu, 12 km (7 miles) northwest of Ninh Binh, was capital of the Dinh dynasty at the end of the 10th century and that of the Earlier Le at the beginning of the 11th. The ruined citadel is not particularly interesting, but the temples dedicated to emperors Dinh Tien Hoang (11th century) and Le Hoan (12th century) are worth a closer look.

From Hanoi to Ha Long

The best route from Hanoi to Ha Long Bay is the so-called "ferry road", which crosses several branches of the Red River by bridge and causeway. The 50 km (31 miles) separating Haiphong from Ha Long are totally enchanting, even though the picturesque old ferries have been replaced by modern bridges and causeways. You cross the Red River right in the centre of Haiphong. On the far bank, you plunge into a different world: almost without transition, the trappings of industry give way to a verdant landscape of paddy fields. Bicycles and porters, heavily laden with fruit, vegetables and poultry, enliven the roads. This bustling population owes its economic life entirely to the sea and the cultivated fields.

The huge limestone rocks of Ha Long Bay appear at the end of the road, where they are beautifully reflected in the waters of the rice fields. Peasants and water-buffalo alike paddle in the mud, setting the stage for the vista which opens out to the sea at Bai Chay.

Haiphong

This route to the bay inevitably takes you to Haiphong, second port and third city of Vietnam after Ho Chi Minh City and Hanoi. A French naval base was once here in what is now a largely commercial and industrial city. Some colonial buildings, notably the station and the Opera House, still remain.

The **Hang Kenh Communal House** has some beautiful wooden sculptures on show. To the south of the town centre, the **Du Hang Pagoda** dates from the Ly Dynasty and is one of the oldest in the country.

Do Son

The sandy beaches of Do Son lie 20 km (12 miles) southeast of Haiphong. A peninsula with a scattering of islets in a pleasant tropical setting, it was formerly a holiday resort for French expatriates. Today the town's beaches, popular for their massage and karaoke facilities, attract crowds from Hanoi and Haiphong.

A junk explores the unique and magical Ha Long Bay.

Cat Ba

The big island of Cat Ba rears up out of the sea only 24 km (15 miles) east of Haiphong. Cat Ba Town, at the western tip, is a busy fishing port as well as a magnet for trippers from the mainland cities. The eastern half of the island is a National Park, much of it forested, with many rare plants. There are a few trails, but poorly marked, so trekkers are recommended to take a guide as well as plenty of water and insect repellent. Otherwise, take a boat trip around southern Ha Long Bay.

Bai Chay

It took only a few years for this ancient fishing village, the western part of Ha Long town, to evolve into a full-blown tourist resort. It could hardly be otherwise: Ha Long Bay, one of the loveliest places in the world by any standards, lies at its doorstep, sprinkled with more than 3,000 small islands whose sheer cliffs rise high up from the sea. Boat excursions take you round this gigantic sculpture gallery.

Ha Long Bay

To absorb all the magic of Ha Long, you have to spend at least two nights in Bai Chay or Hon Gai, the eastern sector of Ha Long town, reached by a bridge over an arm of the sea. Leave the port an hour before dawn to see the sun rise over the bay in a dazzling display of gold and purple. It takes a good day to sail around the most beautiful of the natural formations of the archipelago. The cruise ends at twilight, when the limestone rocks of Ha Long catch fire in the setting sun.

Islands and Caves

The classic cruise takes in the Island of Marvels and its cave Hang Dau Go (Wooden Stakes), three chambers festooned with stalagmites and stalactites; Bo Nau (Pelican Cave); Trinh Nu (The Virgin's Cave); Dong Hang

Hanh tunnel; the island of Bo Hon (Surprise); the Pierced Rock and last but not least, the floating island of Ho Ba Hang (the Three Caverns); with its circle of sugar loaf hills, its caves and craggy cliffs it is considered the single most spectacular site of Ha Long.

The shores of Hon Gai (Sharp Peak), close to the market and the fishing harbour, provide some equally fine panoramas of the bay. The fishermen and market traders crowding around the stalls add a lively human interest.

Northern Region

Living along the Chinese and Laotian borders, Vietnam's 54 ethnic minority groups form a world of their own. Most of these peoples, pushed southwards by the Han colonization, fled China centuries ago and headed for the "land of contrary roads". The minorities are a puzzle for ethnologists. Their domain knows no frontiers, stretching into China, Laos and Cambodia, spilling into Thailand and Myanmar. Even the best Vietnamese guides, enthusiastic and knowledgeable about cultural matters, are not always able to recognize the races with precision. The only way to distinguish them in some cases is by certain details of their clothing. A good number of these communities have managed to preserve their language and traditions.

The Kinh, the majority of the plains who introduced the techniques of rice production and land irrigation, have cultural connections with the mountain-dwelling minorities. They share certain religious beliefs, and there are similarities in their language.

The Meo Zao. The sixth-largest minority of China with almost 6 million members (recorded as the Miao people in the census), the Meo Zao (or Dao) were driven out of their homeland in central Asia at the time of the great Han expansion. They are now found scattered thinly throughout the whole of South-East Asia. They are slowly abandoning their slash-and-burn cultivation methods for more conventional agriculture, an evolution that is leading them toward a more sedentary lifestyle.

The Meo Zao are a minority people with rather sophisticated traditions. The various communities share a common origin but do not necessarily resemble each other. However, one feature they do share is their painstaking concern over beautifying themselves. The women adorn themselves with a king's ransom in silver jewellery, but some of their customs are less attractive to Western eyes—the Vietnamese Zao, for example, protect their teeth with a spectacular coat of black lacquer.

Access to the mountain villages is easy, provided you are ready to forego the usual comforts of the traditional hotel. Bamboo channels supply water for domestic purposes and for irrigating the paddy fields. You can also encounter some of these minority tribes at the markets of Lang Son and Cao Bang, or along the tarred roads leading to these two cities. However, anywhere with access to motor vehicles or television, these people are now becoming "Vietnamized".

Lang Son
Set in a landscape of paddy fields only 18 km (11 miles) from the Chinese border, more than 200 km (124 miles) north of Hanoi, Lang Son was sacked by Chinese troops during their brief 1979 incursion. Encountering stiff resistance, the Chinese alone counted more than 20,000 dead. The town lies at a strategic point on the road and railway leading to Guangxi Province. The frontier was reopened in 1992 to foreigners wishing to see both countries during the same holiday; however, you will need a visa. Cross-border trade is booming, and Ky Lua market is full of Chinese imports as well as local produce and ethnic clothing and crafts. The **Tam Thanh Pagoda**, set in one of a number of grottoes near the town, is also worth a visit.

Cao Bang
There's little of interest in town, but the mountains, grottoes, lakes and waterfalls of **Ba Be National Park**, inhabited by the Dai and Zao peoples, are sufficient reason to make an expedition (by four-wheel drive vehicle) into the countryside. You can view the abundant bird life, take boat trips on Vietnam's largest natural lake and visit its islands.

Hang Pac Bo
On the border with China, two hours' drive from Cao Bang, Pac Bo cave, in a rugged mountainside, was briefly the home of Ho Chi Minh when he entered Vietnam in 1941 to organize resistance against the French. He named the nearby river Lenin and a mountain Karl Marx. Memorabilia have been installed in the new Ho Chi Minh Museum.

Sa Pa
Another place to meet ethnic peoples is the hill station of Sa Pa, founded in 1918 by French colonists. At an altitude of 1,600 m, it lies at the foot of Fan Si Pan, the country's highest peak at 3,143 m.

Three trains per night link Hanoi with the Chinese frontier. There is also a less comfortable-day train. The railway line follows the Red River, cutting through spectacular landscapes and ending at the border town of Lao Cai. From there, you can wind your way by bus or taxi through the countryside to Sa Pa some 30 km (19 miles) away. The Hmong, Zao and Yao people who inhabit this region are very friendly. Walkers will enjoy the steep 9-km (5-mile) hike to the top of Fan Si Pan.

Dien Bien Phu

From Sa Pa to Dien Bien Phu it's a hard day's drive on twisting roads; some travellers prefer to break the journey with a night's stop at Lai Chau, a former provincial capital. An alternative to the road journey is the rapid air shuttle that flies several times a week between Hanoi and Dien Bien Phu, but then you will miss out on the wonderful scenery along the way which includes the stilt houses of Tai farmers; the Hmong live higher in the hills.

History and military enthusiasts come to Dien Bien Phu to see the battleground where the French war in Indochina was finally lost. It was here that the French Army, completely surrounded by the forces of the Vietminh, was obliged to surrender on May 7, 1954 after a siege that lasted 57 days. Fifteen thousand French soldiers had been posted to this valley to deny the Vietnamese troops access to Laos. In December 1953, 50,000 men of

The dress of the Flower Hmong women is the most colourful of all the ethnic minorities.

the Vietminh, commanded by General Vo Nguyen Giap, began their encircling movement. The attack on Dien Bien Phu was launched on March 13, 1954. To the surprise of the French, the Vietnamese were equipped with artillery and subjected the defenders to a ceaseless bombardment. It is estimated that over 3,000 French soldiers were killed whilst the Vietnamese nevertheless suffered losses of more than 20,000. The final number of casualties will probably never be known.

The true scale and significance of the siege and of the Vietnamese victory can be seen by studying the 120 tonne Tuong Dai Chien Dien Bien Phu Memorial erected in 1984 at the north end of town to commemorate the victims lying beneath the paddy fields. The Victory Museum is currently closed.

Thien Mu Pagoda in Hue sits overlooking a pond of blossoming lotus flowers.

The Centre

History has endowed Vietnam with a spine in the shape of the Mandarin Road linking North to South and, in particular, Hanoi to Ho Chi Minh City.

Mandarin Road

Renamed Colonial Road No. 1 by the French, and now simply National Road No. 1A, it was the historic "express" route of the Mandarins from China to the Mekong delta. A vital thoroughfare paralleled by a railway line, the Mandarin Road provides a condensed panorama of the country's numerous attractions.

Thanh Hoa

Between Hanoi and Hué, the road passes through Ninh Binh, in the Hoa Lu region described on p. 24. North of Thanh Hoa, the strategic bridge of Ham Rong, carrying both the road and the railway line, was bombed on several occasions between 1965 and 1972 by the US Air Force.

Thanh Hoa, a quiet little town some 60 km (37 miles) south of Ninh Binh, is a centre for excursions to see the fishermen on stilts and the fine sandy beaches of Sam Son 15 km (9 miles) to the southeast.

At the nearby village of **Dong Son**, jewellery, bronze drums and other objects from one of Asia's oldest civilizations have been discovered. These treasures are on display in museums in Hanoi, Ho Chi Minh City—and as far away as Paris.

Lam Son

Le Loi, who forced back the Chinese in 1427, was born in Lam Son, 50 km (30 miles) northwest of Thanh Hoa. Here you'll see remains of the citadel of Lam Kinh, tombs of the Le rulers and the temple housing the bronze statue of Emperor Le Loi. A stele proclaiming his victory over the Ming dynasty stands at the edge of the lake.

The ruins of the 14th century **Ho Dynasty Citadel** are in the neighbouring village of Tay Giai; the site is UNESCO listed.

South to Vinh

Road No. 1 south of Thanh Hoa, as far as the outskirts of Hué, is rich with historic sites and traces of the Vietnam War, each with its tragic or glorious memories of bombardment, napalm attacks and massacres. Nature is slowly recovering its former beauty. The mountains of Annam sweep down to the sea, and the road winds through stately forests offering fine sea views. Local inhabitants produce attractive pottery and raise silkworms.

Vinh, the provincial capital, is of little interest—the region is one of the poorest in the country—except for its role as birthplace of many men of letters and revolutionaries. Yet only 20 km (12 miles) away are magnificent white sands and the fishing village of **Cua Lo**, where you can sample local seafood and see how *nuoc mam*, a fermented fish sauce, which accompanies many dishes, is made.

Kim Lien

If you are keen to see some Ho Chi Minh memorabilia, you can, like the Vietnamese pilgrims, make the 15-km (9-mile) detour west of Vinh to the valley of the Lam River and the village of Kim Lien, his birthplace and childhood home. Ho's house, now a museum, stands in a garden near a lotus pond.

Hoanh Son

South of Ha Tinh, the Hoang Son mountain chain stretches from Laos to the sea. This natural barrier which rises to about 1,000 m above sea-level, is crossed by way of the Deo Ngang pass which separates Tonkin from Annam, the "Dominion of the South", which the Vietnamese took from the Cham people in the latter part of the 10th century. This rugged frontier, which once separated the empires of China and India, today simply divides the provinces of Ha Tinh and Quang Binh.

Phong Nha

Close to the village of Bo Trach and 25 km (15 miles) from Dong Hoi, a fishing port and capital of Quang Binh Province, the grotto of Phong Nha is hidden in a landscape of conical hills. It comprises several caverns bristling with stalactites and stalagmites; the longest is visited by boat. Remains of Cham altars and inscriptions underline the grotto's use as Buddhist sanctuaries in the 9th and 10th centuries. Upstream, divers have discovered a vast network of tunnels and caves, including the biggest cave in the world, Son Doong, which is over 120 km (74 miles) deep and can not be visited. The group is part of the **Phong Nha-Ke Bang National Park**, a UNESCO Heritage Site.

Demilitarized Zone

From 1954 to 1975, the Ben Hai River was the frontier between North and South Vietnam, separated by a Demilitarized Zone, or DMZ. It has become a place of pilgrimage for war veterans and other political and military strategy buffs. Both parts of the reunified country are linked by the **Hien Luong Bridge**.

In the **national cemetery of Truong Son**, row upon row of gravestones stretch to infinity; they represent some of the 300,000 soldiers of Vietnamese origin declared missing in action.

The **tunnels of Vinh Moc**, symbolic of the resistance, were constructed in horrifying conditions, 24 hours per day for 18 months, to protect against American bombardments. A network of passages between 12 m and 23 m were tunnelled out over three floors by resistance fighters as a storehouse for arms and provisions destined to supply their forces in the South. Many families also lived here permanently. Don't venture inside the tunnels if you suffer from claustrophobia.

Nearby, in startling contrast, you can relax and swim at the splendid palm-fringed beaches.

Made from plaited palm leaves, conical hats are light and resistant, protect from heat and rain, and are worn by everyone from workers in rice paddies to stallholders and women in business suits.

Ho Chi Minh Trail

When the Americans established the McNamara Line, an impenetrable electronic barrier, the North Vietnamese opened the Ho Chi Minh Trail through the Annamite Cordillera and Laos. They transported weapons, munitions and provisions along it to their allies in the South. Tens of thousands of soldiers died in this huge sector along Road No. 9. It is scattered with military bases: Doc Mieu, Con Thien, Camp Carroll and Khe Sanh (now indicated on maps as Huong Hoa). Thousands of US marines were stationed here; their mission was to disrupt movement through the DMZ and along the Ho Chi Minh Trail. In 1968, North Vietnamese forces surrounded and attacked Khe Sanh, in a prelude to the Tet Offensive. Massive aerial bombing just saved the Americans, who later pulled out to avoid their own version of Dien Bien Phu.

Hué

The splendid Imperial City of Hué, ancient Phu Xuan, capital of Annam, comprises the most fascinating historical sites in Vietnam. Some of them are in the citadel, others in the surrounding countryside, which mainly consists of rice paddies.

Built on the banks of Huong Giang, the Perfume River, on an ancient Cham settlement, Hué reflects the might and magnificence of the Nguyen dynasty, in

The Gate of Humanity, one of ten entrances in the walls of the Imperial City.

power from the beginning of the 19th century to the end of French colonization, when it was a hotbed of intellectuals and artists—poets, painters and musicians. Its architecture is inspired by Chinese theories of creation and is harmoniously integrated into the landscape. The five sacred mountains forming a backdrop to the city represent the five elements.

Devastated and pillaged on countless occasions, notably by the French in 1885 and during the Tet Offensive in 1968, the Imperial City has nevertheless retained some remarkable monuments. The ongoing restoration campaign led by UNESCO has brought back their earlier lustre to the luxurious palaces, temples and pavilions, while many ruined monuments have been rebuilt.

Hué cooking is one of the most renowned in the whole country: restaurants and food stalls serve the local specialities—crisp pancakes, spicy noodles and tasty snacks wrapped in banana leaves.

Citadel

Protected by around 10 km (6 miles) of ramparts and a moat 40 m wide, the citadel was built between 1804 and 1832 under the reigns of Gia Long and Minh Mang. Its three concentric enclosures symbolize three sources of power. Kinh Thanh, the Capital City, was the domain of the Mandarin hierarchy. Hoang Thanh, the Imperial City, was the closed space where grand official ceremonies and audiences were held. At the heart of the citadel, Tu Cam Thanh, the Forbidden Purple City, was the private sector reserved for the emperor, the imperial family and eunuchs to serve them, and had the finest buildings. Unfortunately, it is the part that suffered the most damage from floods, fires, termites and bombing. The temples, palaces and monuments which still stand or have been restored bear witness to the magnificence of Hué at the beginning of the 19th century, when the Nguyen emperors held sway over a unified Vietnam. Having entered, you can wander around at your will.

Imperial City

Opposite the imposing flag tower of the King's Knight (1809), the massive **Ngo Mon** (Noon Gate) gives access to the Imperial City. The central corridor was reserved for the emperor, the two next to it for the mandarins, and those on the sides for the soldiers and their mounts—horses and elephants. The gateway is topped by the Pavilion of the Five Phoenixes, a grandstand for the emperor to watch various ceremonies unfolding below.

At the centre of a great courtyard of frangipani trees, the shimmering effects of the Golden Waters Pool set off to perfection the Cau Trung Dao, a bridge reserved exclusively for the emperor. Stone tablets on the Great Greetings Esplanade (**Dai Trieu Nghi**) mark the places allotted to the mandarins according to their hierarchy, when they came to offer greetings to the emperor, traditionally seated on his royal throne in the Palace of Supreme Harmony (**Dien Thai Hoa**). Lavishly decorated and carved in red and gold, the palace presents a harmonious ensemble after its skilful restoration by UNESCO.

Several temples devoted to the cult of the Nguyen emperors have survived. In the southwest corner of the Imperial City, the principal **The To Mieu** (Temple of Generations), with ten decorated altars, is dedicated to the shades of almost all the departed rulers of the dynasty. Facing it are nine masterpieces of 19th-century bronze, the dynastic three-legged urns (Cuu Dinh) 2 m high, weighing 1,900 to 2,500 kg (1.9 to 2.5 tons) and symbolizing the might of the Nguyen emperors. Each one is richly ornamented with pictoral reliefs. Immediately behind them is an elegant three-storey pavilion.

Forbidden Purple City

Behind the Palace of Supreme Harmony, a road stretches from the superb Gate of Humanity in the west to that of Virtue (east). Opposite, the ruins of the Forbidden City consist of two Mandarin houses, one of which contains an exhibition of bronzes, ceramics, carved elephant tusks, games, etc. To the east are the restored library and **royal theatre**, where performances of dance and royal opera are held.

Museum of Royal Fine Arts

Situated to the east of the Citadel area, the museum is set in a superb old house. You can admire imperial costumes and magnificent objects made of gold, as well as porcelain, a throne, a sedan chair and other symbols of power.

Pagodas

Hué is also a sacred city and has over a hundred Buddhist temples and shrines. Many are worth visiting, such as **Tu Dam Pagoda**; founded by a Chinese Buddhist priest in the 17th century, it is famous throughout the land.

You can take a boat to **Chua Thien Mu**, the Pagoda of the Celestial Old Lady, 4 km (2 miles) west of the citadel on a hill overlooking the Perfume River. It was built by Lord Nguyen Hoang in 1601, in response to the apparition of an old woman. She predicted that a prince would come and build a temple of supernatural significance on the site, in order to ensure the prosperity of the country. The 7-storey octagonal tower was added in 1840 by emperor Thieu Tri. Each of its sides represents a different incarnation of Buddha. At his feet are a bronze bell weighing over 3 tons, cast in 1710, and a marble tortoise, the symbol of longevity, bearing a stele carved with the story of the rise of Buddhism in Hué.

Imperial Tombs

In the luxuriant setting of the Hué hills, south of the Perfume River, the seven tombs of the Nguyen emperors lie scattered among the rice paddies, fields and forest, with their cohorts of buildings, statues and stelae. When the emperors were still alive, these were luxurious residences where each tried to leave his own mark.

The longest-reigning emperor, **Tu Duc** (1848–83), built his mausoleum 7 km (4 miles) from Hué, beside a pond designed for the occasion. A pretty fishing pavilion on stilts is reflected in the water, among the lotus flowers. From there, a flight of steps climbs to the palace where Tu Duc lived with his 104 wives and countless concubines. The prodigious number of his companions was of little value for posterity, however, as he produced no male heirs. Another path leads from the pond to a ceremonial courtyard overlooked by two rows of sculpted mandarins, horses and elephants. It opens onto the octagonal Stele Pavilion containing a stone inscribed with praise of the emperor. Beyond this is a crescent-shaped pond, and finally the elaborately decorated tomb itself, guarded from evil spirits by a protective wall.

The reinforced concrete mausoleum of **Khai Dinh**, to the southeast, was built in the 1920s on the side of a steep hill. Its architecture may take you aback.

Many find it rather kitsch, contrasting too sharply with the peaceful mountain setting. The Honour Courtyard contains a profusion of stone statues of mandarins, horses and elephants. The tomb and shrine of Khai Dinh, at the top of some stairs, has a gilded bronze statue of the emperor on his throne, holding a jade sceptre. These all stand apart from the murals and floors composed of gaudy mosaics made of glass and porcelain fragments. The tomb itself is a riot of exuberant decoration.

In the middle of a pine forest, the **Minh Mang Mausoleum**, 12 km (7 miles) from Hué, can be reached by boat along the Perfume River. It is built on a single axis, flanked by two great lakes and outlying pavilions. An esplanade decorated with stone statues links the Salutation Courtyard, the Stele Pavilion and various other temples and pavilions. Beyond it, a second esplanade crosses the Lake of Pure Limpidity by way of three small bridges, leading to three terraces and the emperor's pavilion of eternal rest.

The tomb of **Gia Long**, the first Nguyen emperor, is the furthest from Hué, at around 20 km (12 miles) to the south. Surrounded by mountain peaks and shaded by pine trees, the complex also contains the tombs of members of the imperial family.

Lang Co

Continuing south along the Mandarin Road, you'll come to the fishing village of Lang Co, 68 km (42 miles) from Hué on a spit of sand between the sea and the lagoon. Its long palm-fringed beaches and the delicious seafood will tempt you to stay for a while. The road then climbs to a new 6.2-km tunnel which enables you to bypass **Hai Van**, the Pass of the Ocean Clouds, at 496 m, and save up to an hour on journey time to Hué or Danang. In the 15th century, the pass marked the frontier between Vietnam and the kingdom of Champa.

Danang

In the centre of the country, Danang is one of Vietnam's biggest cities, a major port and the focus of huge expansion and development, including a major land reclamation project for construction of a new town, and ambitious beach resorts undergoing construction. One of its main cultural attractions is the Cham Museum.

Museum of Champa Sculpture

Devoted to the enigmatic Cham civilization, this museum was built in 1915 by the French School of Far-Eastern Studies. The architects were inspired by the Champa towers and temples.

More than 300 objects in terracotta and sandstone have sur-

Danang's Temple of the Marble Mountains, a haven of tranquillity.

vived to testify to the high degree of culture of the Hindu kingdom that occupied the centre of Vietnam as far as the Mekong, and notably the Danang region, after the end of the 2nd century. These decorative objects were only part of the religious architecture — the lintels, tympans and cornerpieces of the temples and towers were ornately sculpted with flowers, leaves, animals and gods.

The exhibits are divided into two periods, before and after the year 1000. Among the great treasures from the 7th to 9th centuries are several sculptures representing the Hindu deities Ganesh, Brahma and Vishnu, an altar to Shiva with scenes recounting the story of Prince Rama, a bevy of seductive dancers, *lingas* (phalluses) and *yonis,* friezes of breasts representing the mother-goddess. The items from the second period are visibly different in style, with animal statues becoming more ornate and those depicting humans less expressive. These artefacts include mythological creatures such as *gajasimha* the elephant-lion, *makara* sea monsters, and *garuda* birds.

Marble Mountains

The most popular excursion from Danang is to the Marble Mountains 10 km (6 miles) south, where hills represent the five elements: Kim: metal, Thuy: water, Moc: wood, Hoa: fire and Tho: earth.

Thuy Son is the highest at 106 m and is pierced with grottoes *(dong)* where the Hindu altars of the Cham have been replaced by Buddhist shrines. **Huyen Khong** is the most spectacular cave, with a height of 35 m. It served as a refuge for Vietnamese soldiers during the war. Four stone spirits watch over this sacred site devoted to the Buddhist, Confucian and Brahman religions. An immense concrete statue of Buddha stands in **Hoa Nghiem Grotto**. As you go back down again, you'll see two pagodas, one of which has a seven-story high stupa.

Hoi An

The port (formerly Faifo) was already open to the world when the first Western traders stopped over in the 16th century, opening up the maritime Silk Route to ivory, mother of pearl, medicinal plants, paper, lacquer, cloth, porcelain, tea, pepper and other spices. In the following century, merchant ships from Portugal, France, Holland, Japan and China turned Hoi An into one of the most significant ports in South-East Asia. A new world was born in its narrow alleys, influenced by Vietnamese traditions and Chinese and Japanese cultures. European missionaries took up residence. But by the 19th century the port had silted up, and Danang took over its role.

UNESCO has recorded more than 850 monuments of historic interest in the little town: wells, bridges, houses, shops, temples, pagodas and tombs. Many of the assembly halls of the brotherhoods (temples) and wooden houses *(hoi quan)* that the Chinese community built here in the late 18th and early 19th centuries have been listed, and some are open for visits. Add a pedestrianised centre, a relic of the colonial district and the charm of its lanterns and Hoi An is almost a living museum.

Alongside the Thu Bon river, near the sampans, the colourful market is the heart of daily life. Here you can buy beautiful materials for bespoke crafting by the town's numerous tailors.

Cau Nhat Ban

This charming covered bridge was built by the Japanese community in 1593 to link its quarter to that of the Chinese. There are statues of 2 dogs at one end and 2 monkeys at the other; they symbolize construction of the bridge beginning in the year of the monkey and ending in the year of the dog. A small pagoda (Chua Cau) was built on the bridge's northern side to protect sailors.

Houses and Temples

Several old houses in the area display a combined Japanese and Chinese influence. Phung Hung has trapdoors installed to enable the inhabitants to lift the furniture upstairs during floods. Many, like the 1802 **chapel-house of the Tran family**, have an ancestral shrine.

The various Chinese communities each built its own assembly hall. Among the most handsome of these, **Phuc Kien**, **Quan Cong** and **Trieu Chau** are protected by a host of Taoist divinities, gryphons, dragons, genies and other mythological heroes. Most of these

superb architectural features are fashioned in openwork wood-carving.

Cua Dai/My Khe

Stretching between Hoi An and Danang, this fine-sand beach (known as Cua Dai in the south and My Khe in the north), is edged by filao trees and pines. More and more international standard hotels are being built in this idyllic setting, but if you want to go bathing, beware of the waves and treacherous currents.

My Son

A mere 30 km (19 miles) separate Hoi An from My Son, the spiritual city of the Champa kingdom from the 4th to the 12th centuries, and the burial place of many of its rulers. Sheltered in a circle of hills, My Son was dedicated to the Hindu deity Shiva. Of its original 68 impressive brick monuments, only 25 are still standing. Having withstood half a millennium of exposure to the elements, they were destroyed in just a few years by American bombing and ground-fighting between the US forces and the Vietcong.

The remains of My Son, capital of the ancient Kingdom of Champa. | The Loris, a small and slow nocturnal primate with huge eyes, is endemic to Vietnam.

Despite recent restoration, the jungle has not yet been cleared from all of the site. First you discover Group C, with its central temple, *kalan*, dedicated to Shiva, representing the universe. The neighbouring Group B claims the most impressive buidings, including a shrine for cult objects that were reserved for the king (B5). Fine reliefs of elephants adorn two of its façades. Of the main *kalan* (B1), only the foundations remain; on them is a *linga* (phallus) on a *yoni* (female principle) with a square base. The nearby Group D is in a pitiful state. However, two buildings have been restored; they contain small collections of reliefs and sculptures.

Inland Route

Instead of following the coast south of Danang, you can head into the Central Highlands, by road or (if short of time) by air. The main towns, Kontum, Pleiku (or Play Ku) and Buon Ma Thuot, are not the chief attractions; they were the scene of heavy fighting in the Vietnam war and have been rebuilt in functional style. Visitors are drawn instead by the chance to meet the locals, by the scenery and the wildlife.

Minority Groups

People of the Bahnar hill tribe live in tall, thatched stilt houses near Kontum; some have been adapted to host groups of trekkers for dinner and overnight stays. Around Pleiku are scattered the villages of the Jarai, such as Plei Boum—another place where visitors are accommodated in stilt houses.

Yok Don National Park

Some 40 km (25 miles) northwest of Buon Ma Thuot, the park includes dry forest typical of South-East Asia, the home of tigers, 200 species of birds, variegated monkeys and elephants, wild and tamed. At **Ban Don** village, near the entrance to the park, you can meet the E De (or Rhade) people, known as skilled elephant trappers and tamers. Some of them still live in extended family groups of up to 40 in traditional longhouses.

Nha Trang

From Hoi An to Nha Trang, the Mandarin Road passes several Cham temples, but it is the coastline beyond Quy Nhon which is chiefly of interest along this route. For 230 km (143 miles) until it reaches Nha Trang, the road passes fishing villages alternating with emerald waters, empty beaches and secret inlets. After the rolling dunes of the **Hon Gom peninsula** you will reach the superb **Doc Let beach** and the white hills of its salt pans, an opportunity to take some fantastic photographs before you arrive at Nha Trang, the friendly capital of Khan Hoa Province.

With 300,000 inhabitants, Nha Trang enjoys a privileged situation on the sea front, beside a natural harbour protected by countless green islands. Thanks to its 8-km (5-mile) beach of fine sand, Nha Trang has become the main seaside resort in the whole of Vietnam. Most water sports can be practised here. In addition, there are several places of cultural or historic interest close to the town centre, and excursions are organized to outlying islands.

Beaches

The beach of **Tran Phu** stretches over 6 km (3 km), offers a wide variety of watersports and forms one of Vietnam's most popular resorts. If you are looking for solitude, nowhere can beat the deserted inlets and virgin strands along the Mandarin Road.

The Harbour

The day begins at 5 a.m. with the arrival in the port of the fishing boats, inevitably accompanied by a great commotion as fishermen cry their wares and stalls are quickly set up on the quayside.

Yersin Museum

At the colonnaded Pasteur Institute on the waterfront, a museum is dedicated to the biologist Alexandre Yersin (1863–1943), where you can see his desk and library. Dr Yersin was born in Aubonne on Lake Geneva, Switzerland, and came to Vietnam in 1889 after having worked with Louis Pasteur in Paris. Six years later, in Hong Kong, he discovered the bubonic plague bacterium (now called *Yersinia* in his honour), and shortly afterwards founded the Pasteur Institute of Nha Trang. Yersin introduced the hevea (rubber tree) and the cinchona (the tree from which quinine is extracted) to Indochina.

Bao Dai's villas

At the southern end of Nha Trang's beach, beyond the main hotels, the five villas of Emperor Bao Dai have been converted into a luxury hotel set in a large park. It crowns the top of a hill, enjoying lovely views of the bay and its fishing village.

The **Institute of Oceanography and Aquarium**, built in 1922, has tanks of rays, seahorses, lobsters, turtles and other marine fauna.

Long Son Pagoda

Decorated with dragon mosaics made from shards of glass and pottery, the Long Son pagoda, on the west side of town, recalls the tomb of Khai Dinh at Hué. The sanctuary was built at the start of the 20th century in front of a hill topped with an enormous white

Buddha seated on a lotus flower. Another, in marble, reclines at the side of the path. Memorials honour the monks and nuns who committed self-immolation in protest against the Diem regime.

Po Nagar

Built between the 7th and 12th centuries, the "Lady of the City" is better preserved than most of Vietnam's Cham sites. It stands proudly on a height overlooking the harbour and the fishing port, to the north of town. At its foot stand the massive columns of a royal *mandapa* (meditation room).

Of the ten towers that formed the sanctuary, four have survived. The great Northeast Tower, A or Thap Chinh, covered by a tapering pyramidal roof, is a fine example of Cham architecture. Over the entrance to this *kalan* built in 817 is a dancing Shiva. Inside, a statue of his wife, the goddess Uma, is bathed in a mystic atmosphere perfumed with incense. Each of the other towers, all of them smaller, contain the masculine *(linga)* and feminine *(yoni)* principles. The Northwest Tower (D) is decorated with a splendid relief depicting a woman on an elephant.

Hon Chong

A short walk north of Po Nagar, the promontory of Hon Chong (Husband Rocks), 4 km (2.5 miles) from the town centre, overlooks the clear waters of the South China Sea, with views of the coastal mountains and nearby islands, in particular Hon Do (Red Island) which is crowned by a Buddhist temple.

Cau Da, Island Cruises

The most memorable excursions from Nha Trang call at the islands just off the coast for snorkelling, a visit to a restaurant or just a relaxing day out. There is no lack of choice, as there are 74 islands in Khanh Hoa province alone.

The most popular island, easily accessible and bursting with seafood, is **Hon Mieu**, where you can visit picturesque fishing villages and a gigantic fishery in the open sea. Choose your own fish and seafood from among the 50 varieties on offer, and take your "catch" to one of the small restaurants on stilts along the shore. When the cruise returns at noon, you will find your tuna, lobster, crayfish, crab, and so on, deliciously grilled and seasoned.

Dao Khi (Monkey Island) is inhabited by these chattering creatures. **Hon Tre** (Bamboo) and **Hon Mun** (Ebony) are popular with divers and snorkellers.

Further afield, **Hon Yen**, the Salanganes Islands, are frequented by authorized swallow's nest hunters in winter. Made from the solidified salivary secretions of the swallow, the nests are prized by Chinese gourmets for their bird's-nest soup. During the hunting season the islands are out of bounds to visitors.

Cham Temples

Between Nha Trang and Ho Chi Minh City (Saigon), the Mandarin Road passes through several pretty coastal stretches.

Cam Ranh Bay was a huge US naval base in the Vietnam war, and was later used by the Soviets before the fall of the USSR and the departure of the Russians. Further south, you will notice the silhouettes of Cham temples beside Road No. 1.

Po Klong Garai

From Phan Rang-Thap Cham, 103 km (64 miles) from Nha Trang, turn west onto the Dalat road (No. 20) to reach one of the finest monumental Cham groups, 6 km (4 miles) inland.

Po Klong Garai stands on the crest of a sandstone hill visible from the road. Outlined against the sky, four 13th-century towers on a vast brick esplanade make a striking architectural statement. The entrance is surmounted by a six-armed dancing Shiva. The *kalan* (sanctuary) is decorated with a multitude of statues, some occupying all the niches on the façade and others emerging like bristling gargoyles from every

---

Champa. The people of the kingdom of Champa were of Indonesian origin and spoke a Malayo-Polynesian language, but they became Indianized towards the end of the 2nd century through trade with that great Hindu culture, so attaining a high level of civilization. Their talents were multi-faceted: the seafarers dominated the silk and spice trades, the agricultural specialists produced a fast-growing variety of rice which revolutionized China in the 13th century, and constructors developed hard-wearing brick-building techniques.

King Bhadravarman created the religious centre of My Son in the 4th century, and his successors never stopped embellishing it. The kingdom was feared and respected, but the advent of a new and ambitious Vietnam to the north in the 15th century was destined to transform the country's frontiers. The Great March South of the Vietnamese, the Nam Tien, dismantled the kingdom of Champa in 1471 after taking the capital, Vijaya. Today, the 400,000 thousand Chams of South-East Asia are dispersed among the ethnic minorities of that vast region, but some still remain within Vietnam's borders in Ninh Thuan Province near Phan Rang.

angle of the roof. A carved, six-armed Shiva is carved above the entrance, with inscriptions all around the door-frames.

Beyond the vestibule and its traditional white statue of the bull Nandi, an unusual *mukha-linga* appears beneath a wooden vault, surrounded with offerings and sticks of incense. This stylized phallus symbolizes the virility and creative force of Shiva, and bears, presumably as a gesture of reverence, a painted face thought to be a likeness of King Po Klong Garai, who reigned from 1151 to 1205.

Po Rome

One of the last sanctuaries of Cham civilization, Po Rome (or Ro Me) lies 15 km (9 miles) south of Phan Rang-Thap Cham, on high ground at the end of a 6-km (4-mile) track to the west of Road No. 1. This region is inhabited by large communities of the minority Cham, and you will see many families along the track, which is passable only in dry weather. You will have to park your vehicle and walk for about 10 minutes to reach the hill on which the 16th-century Cham temple stands. Stairways lead to the top.

Inside the temple, the usual symbols of agricultural fertility, two stone statues of white Nandi bulls, stand guard before an altar. Above it is a magnificent bas-relief dedicated to King Po Rome, one of the last Cham rulers (1627–51), deified in the form of Shiva. He died a prisoner of the Vietnamese.

Dalat

The winding scenic mountain road heading inland to Dalat passes through some beautiful countryside. At an altitude of 1,300–1,500 m, Dalat is the capital of Lam Dong Province, where the perpetual spring-like climate offers a different aspect of Vietnam. The hill station owes its reputation to Dr Yersin (see p. 42), who discovered the cool, healthy site in 1893. Some historical sites, those of the Summer Palace of Bao Dai, the last emperor, and a number of early colonial villas continue to attract Europeans, just as at the start of the 20th century. A few kilometres from the centre, the **Valley of Love** and its lake, busy with small boats, the legendary Lake of Sighs, is a favourite honeymoon destination.

Town Centre

Dalat has expanded in a rash of concrete buildings, including **Cho Dalat** the large central market, a popular meeting place for the ethnic groups from the high plateaux. There is usually a photogenic array of foods.

Emperor Bao Dai's golf course on the shores of **Xuan Huong Lake** has been renovated. At the northeast end of the lake, the Flower Garden displays roses, camellias, lilies and other tropical plants, as well as an orchid house.

St Nicholas cathedral, south of the market, has colourful stained-glass windows made in France. It was built from 1931 to 1942.

Pagodas

Northwest of the centre, the **Chua Linh Son Pagoda** (1842), reserved for men only, has a huge bronze and gold bell and is fronted by two dragon balustrades.

South of Dalat, the **Chua Thien Vuong Pagoda**, built in the 1950s by the Chinese community, has three gold-lacquered sandalwood statues, 4 m high, each weighing almost a tonne and a half.

Around Dalat

In the nearby villages you can meet the many tribes of mountain dwellers living in wooden stilt-houses. These include the Lat, Koho, Chill, Ma, and Maug peoples. Continuing northwards to the plateaux of the neighbouring Dac Lac Province, you will encounter other ethnic minorities—and elephants. This most fertile region of the country is rich with coffee farms, flowers and, unusually, locust breeding. You can also visit silk workshops.

Waterfall Road

The journey along Road No. 20 passes through magnificent country with some of the most breathtaking waterfalls in the land. The **Prenn Falls**, 16 m high, are only 13 km (8 miles) from Dalat and make a very popular outing for the Vietnamese.

Even more spectacular, the **Lien Khuong** Falls, 36 km (22 miles) from Dalat, tumble through virgin forest, where the River Da Nhim cascades over a cliff 18 m high.

The **Gougah Falls** are a little further on, about 40 km (25 miles) from Dalat. Follow a track to the left off Road No. 20 and after a 10-minute walk the splendid sight of this natural wonder will come into view, parted at the centre like a curtain by a huge volcanic rock.

The watery spectacle continues with the **Pongour Falls**, 54 km (33 miles), from Dalat and then a further 8 km (5 miles), along a small road.

You can also see the **Bo Bia** Cascade 6 km (4 miles) from Di Linh among the tea plantations, and lastly the **Dambri Falls**, possibly the highest in the country at 90 m. The water plunges into a sink-hole surrounded by tropical vegetation. Access is from Bao Loc by an easy 16 km (10 miles) long road, following through tea and mulberry plantations.

To reach Ho Chi Minh City, the road crosses **Lake Tri An** on a mighty bridge which affords views of picturesque lake houses on stilts, built by fishermen who have settled on this artificial lake abounding in underwater life.

Phan Thiet

The Mandarin Road swings away from the coast before meeting it again at the major fishing port of Phan Thiet, where the quayside market generates an entertaining pandemonium every morning. East of the town is a long arc of south-facing sandy beaches, stretching for most of the 22 km (14 miles) to **Mui Ne**. Near the cape itself the sands turn red and rear up in spectacular dunes. Inevitably, developers were attracted to this piece of shoreline, which looks set to rival Nha Trang as Vietnam's top resort, especially as it's quite accessible from Ho Chi Minh City. There are a number of hotels with water sports facilities. They have become a favourite with tour groups, both for beach holidays and for overnight stops.

These surprising little boats, made from plaited bamboo, are ideal for fishing. | An unmissable photo opportunity at the superb Pongour Waterfalls. | The rising sun casts an orange glow over dunes not far from Mui Ne.

The ornate City Hall complete with central bell tower was completed in 1908.

The South

Vietnam's premier port, Ho Chi Minh City (HCMC), still often called Saigon, is also the largest city in the land. Official figures put the population at 4 million, but if you include the whole metropolitan area, this busy capital sizzling with life actually numbers more than 7 million inhabitants.

Ho Chi Minh City

Born in the 17th century, developed in colonial times, Saigon long ruled over the fate of Cochin China. As efficient as ever, the city is of limited interest to anyone in search of the exotic, but it does have a special atmosphere. The city centre, which can easily be explored on foot, exudes a good atmosphere. A certain nostalgia floats around the big French monuments, confronting a vibrant spirit of enterprise, a hectic rhythm typical of a city undergoing a renaissance.

City Centre

The twin spires of the red-brick neo-Romanesque **Notre Dame cathedral**, built between 1877 and 1880, rise 40 m over a square in the middle of the embassy district. The superb **Central Post Office**, its metal framework designed by Gustave Eiffel, also looks onto the square.

West along Le Duan avenue, **Reunification Hall** (Dinh Thong Nhat), formerly the Presidential Palace, is a concrete replacement built after rebellious South Vietnamese pilots bombed the old one in 1962. It served as the presidential palace until 1975. Not far from there is the **War Remnants Museum**, with helicopters, tanks and bombs in the courtyard. Military atrocities are analysed in graphic and disturbing detail, photographs and exhibits illustrate the inhumanity of mankind.

Southeast of the Presidential Palace is the **Ho Chi Minh City Museum**, in a handsome colonial building, documenting in a terse manner the history of the city. Closer to the centre, the **City Hall**, similar in design to that of Paris, houses the People's Committee. From there you can continue walking southwest, along Le Than Ton avenue, to **Cho Ben Thanh** covered market and the Hindu temple, **Chua Ba Mariamman**, where guardians Maduraiveeran and Pechiamman stand beside the goddess Mariamman, behind two *lingas*.

The **Fine Arts Museum** on Pho Duc Chinh Street contains beautiful Cham sculptures as well as finds from Oc-Eo, a town in the ancient Kingdom of Funan, and many lovely paintings and laquered works. There are also many antique shops in this area.

Leading from the cathedral, **Dong Khoi Road** is lined with hotels and restaurants all the way to the

Saigon River. The **Opera House** (or Municipal Theatre), built at the beginning of the 20th century, is also on this thoroughfare, along with art galleries, souvenir shops, the large stores and the mosque.

The **Song Sai Gon** (Saigon River) which links the city to the sea with 225 km (139 miles) of waterway, is open to craft of all kinds, including floating restaurants that take their passengers to the port and back on gastronomic and musical cruises.

If you follow Le Duan boulevard northwards from the cathedral, you will reach the Botanical Gardens and Zoo. The **Vietnam History Museum**, within the grounds, houses the famous bronze drums from Dong Son and many sculptures and other artefacts from Oc-Eo.

Pagodas

Just north of La Van Tam Park, in the Da Cao district, **Chua Ngoc Hoeng**, the Pagoda of the Jade Emperor, was built in 1909. Its rooms contain a multitude of large papier-mâché statues of warriors, generals and divinities, all drowning in incense fumes. The Taoist Jade Emperor Ngoc Hoang, wrapped in shining red garments, is in the middle of the principal sanctuary, surrounded by his four guardians, the Great Diamonds. In a small chamber, twelve ceramic statues of female

Five appealing pagodas. The most unusual is the **Perfume Pagoda**, a group of twelve sanctuaries set in the magnificent limestone mountains of Ha Tay Province, south of Hanoi. In the east, the **Paintbrush Pagoda** bristles with handsome carved stone monuments. In Hanoi, the pretty **One Pillar Pagoda**, shaped like a lotus, recalls a charming legend. The **Celestial Old Lady Pagoda** in Hué boasts a three-ton bronze bell and a marble tortoise. In Ho Chi Minh City, the **Giac Lam Pagoda** is a fine example of Vietnamese architecture.

flickr.com/Rogers

figures represent the months of the Chinese calendar and symbolize good and bad features of the human character.

Chua Giac Lam, the Forest of Enlightenment Pagoda, 8 km (5 miles) west of the centre, was built in 1744 in typical Vietnamese style and renovated in 1900. As well as its Bodhi tree, it houses many original statues of Buddha, several gilded. Notice the unusual Tree of Wandering Souls, formed out of 49 lamps and statuettes of Buddha. Several times a day, prayer ceremonies accompanied by singing, gongs, bells and drums bring a bit of life to this tranquil temple.

The architecture of **Chua Giac Vien**, Buddha's Complete Enlightenment Pagoda, southwest of Chua Giac Lam, has similar features, down to identical statuary such as the laughing Ameda beckoning little children to him.

Cholon

Southwest of the centre, HCMC's Chinatown is an integral part of the city. Despite the authorities' anti-Chinese campaign of 1978–79, the population of this huge and dynamic quarter, the Hoa, still speak Cantonese or Mandarin and dialects derived from it.

The area is entirely dedicated to commerce—its name means "Great Market"—and there are bazaars all over the place. Not only will you find all Western products, but also, and at lower prices, a profusion of useful and practical goods (medical equipment, Swiss army knives with the white Swiss cross replaced by the Vietnamese star, lighters, spare parts for bicycles, etc.), and a host of items artfully manufactured or salvaged from the detritus of our consumer society.

There are numerous temples here in Chinatown, and several of them are well worth a look: **Ba Thien Hau** for its painted ceramic

istockphoto.com/Bath

Coils of incense hang from a temple roof; in each one is the name of the person for whom they were lit.

The ornate cathedral of the Cao Dai religion in Tay Ninh.

sculptures; **Phuoc An Hoi Quan** for its porcelain miniatures, its sacred objects and the life-size sacred horse of Quan Cong. **Ong Bon** (or Mieu Nhi Phu) boasts a carved wooden altar; **Phung Son Tu** has countless statues; **Tam Son Hoi Quan** is richly decorated. **Khanh Van Nam Vien** is known for its exemplary Taoism; **Ha Chuong Hoi Quan** for its frescoes and the stone pillars carved in China. Last but not least, Quan Am is renowned for the gilded statue of A Pho, the Queen of Heaven, and its roof decorated with ceramics.

The Catholic Church of **Cha Tam** was the last refuge of President Ngo Dinh Diem before his execution in November 1963.

Cholon's market, **Cho Binh Tay**, overflows everywhere onto the street with fruit, vegetables, fish and meat.

Excursions from Ho Chi Minh City

It's worth devoting a whole day to Tay Ninh and the tunnels of Cu Chi, northwest of Ho Chi Minh City. If you're longing for a beach, head for Vung Tau or, even better, Long Hai.

The Tunnels of Cu Chi

Used by the Vietminh and Vietcong in their wars against the French and Americans, the tunnels of Cu Chi are located 50 km (31 miles) from Ho Chi Minh City on the Tay Ninh road. Tour operators usually bring their flocks here as part of an excursion to the Caodaist Holy See. However, the tunnels are mainly of interest to war veterans and students of guerilla warfare, and do not count among the most uplifting attractions of Vietnam.

The three-level complex of tunnels was excavated between 1948 and 1973. They cover a distance of 250 km (155 miles) in total. After a walk through the stuffy, extremely narrow corridors, where you can peer into chambers fitted out as kitchens, dormitories, shelters, hospitals and conference rooms, you tour a small part of the densely booby-trapped 420 sq km (162 sq miles) of terrain, described as the "most devastated, bombarded, defoliated and gassed in the whole history of warfare".

The atmosphere of war is partially recreated by tourists carrying weapons to the firing range.

Tay Ninh

The Holy See of the Cao Dai religion, the third most important in the country after Buddhism and Catholicism, is at Tay Ninh, 100 km (62 miles) northwest of HCMC. This small town, whose inhabitants are mostly Vietnamese with Khmer and Cham minorities, has given its name to the province, which juts into Cambodia.

Founded at the beginning of the 20th century in the village of Long Hoa near Tay Ninh, Caodaism has its spiritual sources in an amalgamation of the best aspects of the great ancient religions of the world, Buddhism, Christianity, Confucianism, Taoism, Hinduism and Islam, coloured by Spiritualism and a touch of opportunism. Caodaism is the prime example of religious syncretism. This openness to all philosophies helps to avoid any forms of fundamentalism.

The Great Temple

In the entrance hall of the Great Temple, a fresco depicts the signatories of the "Third Alliance between God and Man", the three Caodaist saints: Nguyen Binh Khiem (1492–1587), an Annamite poet and man of letters; Victor Hugo (1802–85) in the robes of a member of the French Academy; and Sun Yatsen (1866–1925), the revolutionary and founder of the Republic of China. The alliance ecumenically unites Jesus Christ, Buddha, Mohammed, Confucius, Joan of Arc, Shakespeare, Pasteur, Lenin, Churchill, Descartes and the astronomer Flammarion!

The rococo extravaganza of this holy city, dominated by the Great Temple, takes its inspiration from every architectural style imaginable. Beyond the immense nave, supported by pillars carved with dragons, is the Globe of the Most High, a monumental blue sphere scattered with stars and the "Divine Eye"—the most venerated emblem of Caodaism, symbolizing God.

Above the altar are the six key personages of Caodaoism: Sakayamuni, founder of Buddhism; Ly Thai Bach, a fairy of Chinese mythology; Khuong Tu Nha, the Chinese saint Jiang Taigon; Lao Tse, the founder of Taoism; Quan Cong, the Chinese god of war (Guangong); and Quan Am, the Chinese goddess of mercy (Guanyin). Ceremonies take place four times a day, every six hours. The principal service starts at noon, when the excursion groups from HCMC have delivered their busloads to fill the galleries. Cardinals, priests, deacons and other male and female dignitaries, in mandarin-style robes, enter in procession along the great nave. They are grouped according to the colour of their robes, with men on one side and women on the other. In the upper gallery, a choir sings hymns, accompanied by an orchestra. Now and then, women in the centre of the nave sing and beat wooden drums.

With its dazzling cathedral-pagoda and the choreography of participants in bright robes, the Holy See of Tay Ninh is an undeniable tourist attraction. A pilgrimage here can be rounded off by a trip to the beautiful surrounding countryside planted with rubber trees and to the tunnels of Cu Chi.

Vung Tau

Only its proximity to Ho Chi Minh City 120 km (75 miles) away accounts for the reputation of Vung Tau as a seaside resort. The beaches, cliffs and temples of the former French beach retreat of Cap Saint-Jacques are not without their attractions, but the nearby construction of the vast international port of Sao Mai and the exploitation of rich offshore deposits of oil and gas could well wipe out any holiday-geared expansion.

The beach at **Long Hai**, 40 km (25 miles) away on the Ho Chi Minh City road, is extremely beautiful, quieter and with finer sand than Vung Tau; several luxury resorts have been developed there.

The Mekong Delta

Flowing from Cambodia, the Mekong enters Vietnam at the border town of **Vinh Xuong** then widens into a delta region covering some 64,000 sq km (25,000 sq miles). It is known locally as "Cuu Long"—the Nine-Dragon River—a reference to its various branches at this point—nine main channels and countless creeks, where land and water intertwine. To the south and west of Ho Chi Minh City, this vast, flat landscape makes up 10 per cent of the country's area but produces almost 40 per cent of the rice crop. This intensive agriculture is a relatively recent development; the effort of taming the floods and tides was not thought to be worthwhile until the French colonial period. Aquaculture also represents a large part of the production of freshwater fish.

A road journey through the delta is continually interrupted by the necessity of waiting for fer-

THE MIGHTY MEKONG

The third-longest river in Asia (4,350 km, or 2,700 miles), the Mekong rises in the highlands of Tibet and empties into the sea at the extreme south of Vietnam, having irrigated the Chinese provinces of Szechwan and Yunnan, and Myanmar, Laos, Thailand and Cambodia along the way. The Vietnamese call it Song Cuu Long, the Nine Dragons River, these being the nine branches of the famous delta, the rice bowl of the country. The last region to be conquered and annexed by Vietnam, the delta belonged to the Khmer kingdom until the 18th century.

The river reaches its highest level in September. Like the Red River, its continual deposit of silt extends the shoreline by 70 to 100 m into the South China Sea each year. The land is so low-lying that the twice-daily tides can reach as far as 300 km (186 miles) inland.

By a curious natural peculiarity, the immense Cambodian lake Tonle Sap, which empties into the Mekong at Phnom Penh, sees the course of the river reverse during periods of flooding, which allows it to hold back enough water to prevent dramatic inundation in the delta region. However, the deforestation of Cambodia is imperilling this ecological balance. An increase in the salt water flowing in from the sea could have serious consequences for the fertility of the land. As well as rice, the Mekong delta produces many fruits and vegetables, notably sugar cane, mangoes and coconuts.

istockphoto.com/Balestri

Bundles of incense, produced in the Mekong delta region.

ries, but there's plenty to see while you wait. An even better way of travelling is to take a boat trip, to see the floating markets and the amazing variety of craft and cargoes. The delta is abundant in fruit. The sampans that cross the various tributaries, especially at Vinh Long and Can Tho, carry melons, bananas and durians to the markets, contributing to the general hustle and bustle of life on the river. Cruises from Cambodia or even higher upriver in Laos end at My Tho, and shorter excursions can also be arranged from Vinh Long.

The marshiest regions and mud flats covered at high tide are a paradise for wading birds and virtually inaccessible to humans. Closest to the sea, thick curtains of mangroves border vast expanses of water where the silence is disturbed only by the shrieks of birds and the slither of crocodiles. The humid horizons of the Mekong delta provide an astonishing variety of landscapes, but however idyllic, they remain at the mercy of thoughtless human exploitation, pollution and hydrological disturbance.

Tan Chau

Also called Phu Chau, the town 20 km (12 miles) inside the border is set within vibrant green rice paddy fields. Tan Chau is known as a centre for handicrafts, most notably in silk, and you might have the possibility of visiting a silk-weaving factory here.

The Hau Giang branch of the river flows past **Chau Doc**, where many Cham, Khmer and Chinese live; each community has its own temple. The economy here depends largely on fish farming, and the town is famous for its variety of fish sauces. Excursions are arranged to visit a Cham minority village where you can see how the people live and work.

Mount Sam, 5 km (3 miles) southwest of Chau Doc, is no more than a hill, but it rises steeply from the vast green chequerboard of rice paddies and offers good views of the delta and into Cambodia. The hillside is scattered with pagodas, grottoes and an assortment of "attractions" intended to appeal to the many local visitors. They flock especially to the gaudy Tay An Pagoda near the foot of the hill, filled with colourful statuary.

Can Tho

The largest city of the delta on the Hau Giang branch, this is the epicentre of the region, a busy town with a buzzing waterfront. It is the best base for excursions around the delta. The hotel infrastructure is excellent, the floating market at **Cai Rang** (half an hour by boat) is alone worth the journey—as is that at **Phung Hiep**—and

the roads and waterways together offer rapid access to all the other attractions of the Mekong.

In town, the **Can Tho Museum** describes the history of local resistance during foreign rule and documents the culture and history of the province.

The Buddhist **Munirangsyaram Pagoda** with its highly ornamented façade, serves the local Khmer community and features a figure of Buddha beneath a Bodhi tree. Facing the river, **Chua Ong**, a temple set inside the Guangzhou Assembly Hall, was built in the 19th century for the ethnic Chinese population, though most of them fled after persecutions in the late 1970s. The temple was designed to represent the Chinese character for "nation". In the centre is a figure of Kuang Kung, a deity symbolizing many merits including justice and courage. He is flanked by the God of Earth and the God of Finance.

To relax after your trip along the river, call in at **Van Tho 2**, where professional blind therapists can give you a wonderful, traditional Vietnamese or Japanese massage.

You have to get up very early to see the best of the floating markets—the activity is at its height at around 5am. All sorts of products are on sale, from fish to flowers to dragon fruit.

Excursions from Can Tho

A road leads west from Can Tho to the Gulf of Thailand. The port of **Rach Gia**, with its markets and superb pagodas, is home to large numbers of Khmer and Chinese. In the dry season, it is possible to visit the site of the ancient city of **Oc-Eo**. The principal artefacts to have been unearthed are on display in the History Museum and Fine Arts Museum in Ho Chi Minh City.

The excursion continues north along the gulf to **Ha Tien**. The coastline is wonderful, with unspoilt beaches stretching as far as the Hon Chong Peninsula, caves transformed into temples, and small islands like the heavenly Nghe or the hilly Phu Quoc.

Another one- or two-day circuit from Can Tho will appeal mainly to birdwatchers. Heading southwards, it includes **Soc Trang**, with its Khmer Museum and a Bat Pagoda; **Bac Lieu** and its bird sanctuary and Khmer Pagoda; and **Ca Mau**, hidden away in the mangrove forest of U Minh. Ca Mau is of interest for the Ngoc Hien ornithological nature reserve, but be aware of its mosquito-infested marshes and go armed with plenty of repellent. Among the endemic birds are several kinds of laughing thrush, the crested argus, the white-eared night heron and the Vietnamese greenfinch.

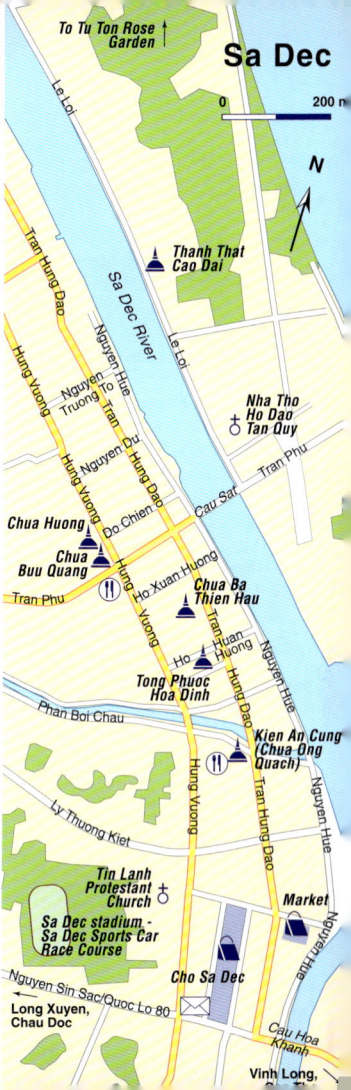

Sa Dec

On the Tien Giang branch of the river, picturesque Sa Dec retains the flavour of its colonial past as recorded in the work of a former resident, the novelist Marguerite Duras. The daughter of French colonists, she was born in Saigon in 1914 and lived in Sa Dec, where her mother ran a school, from 1928 to 1932. Her love affair with Huynh Thuy Le, the son of a wealthy Chinese family, forms the basis of her novel *The Lovers*, which won the Goncourt prize in 1984. The Chinese family home is at 225A Nguyen Hue St on the east bank of the Sa Dec River, across from the main market. It is a fine example of colonial architecture — but apparently Marguerite herself never went there. Guided tours are available in English and French.

Back in the centre of town, the classic form of the **Chua Huong Tu pagoda** marks the Chinese influence in Vietnamese culture. Sa Dec's most popular sight, though, is its famous **flower nurseries** north of the centre. These supply the markets of Ho Chi Minh City and are especially busy on Sundays and during the Tet festival in January-February. That of nearby **Vuon Hong Tu Ton Rose Garden** plays host to more than 500 different types of rose.

Almost opposite Sa Dec, the region is known for its role during the Vietnam War. Located in the middle of the forest was the secret **Xeo Quyt** base, where senior Vietcong officers directed the campaign against the Americans from within submerged metal containers. They carried this out in remarkably close proximity to the US army's own heartland around Saigon (Ho Chi Minh City) and, suspicious, the Americans frequently bombed the forest but never located them. Today, a boat tour of the narrow channels, through dense forest and past preserved bunkers and old minefields, gives a powerful sense of what the Vietcong experienced in the 15 years of war spent here until final victory in 1975.

Further north, **Tram Chim National Park** is a huge flooded area, inhabited by numerous species of fish and birds, including several kinds of cranes.

Vinh Long

Around 20 km (12 miles) to the southeast and situated on the Cu Chien River, one of the branches of the Mekong delta, the provincial capital of Vinh Long is a noisy town with an atmospheric waterfront, especially along **Phan Boi Chau Road**, whose prettier cafés and restaurants offer respite from the hustle and bustle of the centre. On the same street, **Vinh Long Museum** focuses on the history and culture of the region, while the section concerned with the Vietnam War will grab the attention for its graphic record of the horrors of that conflict.

The **Van Thanh Mieu Temple** is 3 km (2 miles) southeast of Vinh Long. Dating from the mid-19th century, it is dedicated to Confucius, a considerable rarity in southern Vietnam. In the front is a memorial to Phan Thanh Gian, (Vietnamese Ambassador to France during the 1860's, who committed suicide when French tropps invaded the southern provinces of Vietnam). However, the most popular features of Vinh Long are its delightful river islands, such as **An Binh** and **Binh Hoa Phuoc**. These calm, watery landscapes are interlaced by small canals and, with their stilt houses and lush fruit trees, are wonderful places for a relaxing cruise.

Cai Be

Not far from Vinh Long, on the Mekong itself, the Cai Be **floating market** is a huge draw for locals and tourists alike. Although the wares on sale are not that unusual—delicious local vegetables and fruits such as melon, durian

A local curiosity: snake wine (where turtles, insects or worms may also be steeping). | Visits to the floating markets involve walking up and down narrow bridges.

The ornate Vinh Trang Pagoda in My Tho is a combination of many different architectural styles.

and banana—it's the manner of shopping that's novel, as every part of the transaction is conducted on the water: stallholders sell from larger boats, hanging out tasting samples from poles to wholesalers, while shoppers mill about on smaller craft. It all takes place against the backdrop of Cai Be's 19th-century French Gothic **cathedral**, whose elegant white spire dominates the river.

My Tho

A further 40 km (25 miles) brings you to My Tho, an important trading town with streets set out in a grid pattern on the north bank of the Mekong. Its bustling river traffic is best seen from **Lac Hong Park**, a popular local meeting place with a statue of Nguyen Huu Huan, a celebrated 19th-century opponent of French colonial power who lived in the town. Head northwards and you will soon arrive at the huge **central market**. Its myriad stalls fill the streets and sell an interesting range of fishing and boating paraphernalia along with mounds of fruit, tobacco and other items.

Across the Bao Dinh Canal is the small Chinese district. My Tho was founded in the late 17th century by Chinese exiles from Taiwan. Today, there is little trace of them, though it's an intriguing area to stroll around. A short walk to the north, the **Vinh Trang Pagoda** has an impressively ornate façade in a mixture of Southeast Asian and French styles that gives way to an attractive interior decorated with glazed tiles and gilt work. It was built in 1849. Donations are welcomed by the monks who provide a home for orphans and other needy children.

The nearby river islands are also worth exploring. Boat trips might include visits to a coconut candy workshop, potteries, brickworks, an orchid garden or a bee farm. **Con Phung** (Phoenix Island) was home to the "Coconut Monk", a hermit born Nguyen Thanh Nam in 1909, who came here in 1945 to meditate and who allegedly lived on nothing but coconuts for three years. He wore a crucifix and traditional Buddhist robes. Unfortunately, his more public meditations on the reunification of Vietnam after World War II meant that he was regularly imprisoned by the South Vietnamese government.

Beautiful **Con Tan Long** (Dragon Island) is known for its longan orchards and coconut trees lining the beach, while **Thoi Son** (Unicorn Island) is popular for its atmospheric channels and their palm canopies, as well as the production of banana wine.

From My Tho, the Mekong flows for just 50 km (30 miles) more before emptying out into the South China Sea.

Handmade masks in a variety of demure smiles and toothy grins.

SHOPPING

The opening of the country to foreign tourists has given local artisans a new lease of life. The ethnic minorities are skilled at all kinds of colourful crafts.

Ceramics
Pottery, porcelain and ceramics with designs in cobalt blue on a white background are widely available in every shape and size. Bowls, saucers, chopstick holders and so on fit easily into your luggage. It may be more difficult to take home a multicoloured elephant or statuettes of Buddhist divinities.

Fabrics
Magnificent embroidery in shimmering colours brightens up sheets, pillowcases and tablecloths. Tailors can produce made-to-measure suits and dresses in 48 hours. The ladies' *ao-dai* can be made to order, though it is also available more cheaply off the peg.

Lacquerware
The art of lacquering originated in neighbouring China, and is carried on today in time-honoured fashion. Genuine lacquer is the sap of the tree *Rhus vernicifera*, native to the Far East, which is extracted and left to oxidize and harden in the open air. This results in a liquid as thick as syrup. A coat of lacquer is applied over each layer of colour: the most beautiful antique items can have up to two hundred layers.

Silk
The favourite subjects for silk painting are scenes from daily life in the villages and fields. Pastel shades depict the changing colours of the seasons, with the texture of the silk lending a hint of romanticism. Glued to a paper backing, the pictures are easy to transport flat at the bottom of a suitcase.

Yet More Souvenirs
Prints, engravings, leather goods, wooden carvings, green tea and spices are bound to satisfy the most ardent shopaholic. Collectors will probably like to browse among old stamps, coins, medals and military surplus (very often brand-new "aged" copies), and amazing copies of Old Masters.

Unusual ingredients for the cooking pot in Vietnam's fascinating markets.

DINING OUT

Many Vietnamese dishes are variations on the great Chinese gastronomic tradition. The similarity ends when it comes to the way certain ingredients are used. Vietnamese cuisine is spicier than southern Chinese, and contains great quantities of green vegetables and aromatic herbs. The technique lies in rapid cooking—in broth, by steaming or by stir-frying.

Nuoc mam

The national seasoning, *nuoc mam*, or fish sauce, plays the same role as soy sauce. It is produced by packing fish into jars between layers of salt and letting it all ferment. Diluted with water or lemon juice, and enhanced with chilli or sugar (when it is called *nuoc cham*), *nuoc mam* is served with every meal, either separately as a seasoning or added during cooking.

Rice and bread

Vietnam is a major producer of rice (fifth on a world scale) and a great consumer: it is the staple of the daily diet and served at every meal. The fertile deltas of the Mekong and the Red River produce two or three rice harvests per year, composed of four different varieties. Rice flour is the main ingredient of transparent thread noodles and of rice pancakes too.

A legacy of colonial days, the French *baguette* is to be found in every marketplace and on every restaurant table.

Soups and snacks

Pho, which originated in the North, is a soup of transparent thread noodles enriched with beef or chicken or other things, and is flavoured with *nuoc mam*, lemongrass, ginger, coriander or spices. This cheap and popular dish is served at all hours of the day from impromptu street stalls that lure you with the delicious cooking smells. The equivalent in the South is *hu tieu*, a soup of pork or crab and shrimp.

Another traditional dish is *goi*, a term encompassing various salads and raw vegetables (not for delicate stomachs!) topped with thinly sliced meat and garnished with coconut, peanuts and fried onion.

Familiar specialities in many Chinese and Vietnamese restaurants in the West are spring rolls, called *nem* in the North and *cha gio* in the South. It consists of a fine rice-flour pancake wrapped around a tasty filling of crab, pork, thread noodles, onions and mushrooms. They are deep-fried and served on a bed of salad, to be enjoyed with the indispensable *nuoc mam* and fresh mint leaves. *Cuon* (spring rolls) are prepared with thin, raw rice pancakes and come filled with meat, prawns, noodles and freah mint.

Meat and Fish
Stock-rearing is uncommon in Vietnam. Beef *(bo)* and lamb are expensive and generally imported from Australia. On the other hand, pork *(lon)* figures more frequently on menus, along with chicken *(ga)* and duck *(vit)*.

The rivers and streams produce an abundance of freshwater fish and crustaceans, and the South China Sea delivers up a fresh harvest daily: shrimp *(tom)*, crab *(cua)*, shellfish and fish of all sorts. Among the many specialities is the Hanoi favourite *cha ca*, fish grilled with aromatic herbs and accompanied by rice noodles and peanuts. In the south, coconut milk is often used.

Desserts
Rice is often one of the ingredients used in the preparation of sweet dishes such as *banh com*, where a portion of rice is stuffed with bean paste and coconut. Another such dish is *banh deo*, a cake of rice flour, sesame seeds and candied fruits. Baked custards *(che)* are widespread, prepared with soya cheese, maize, coconut milk and lotus seeds.

Drinks
Green tea is the national drink and is often served at meal times. Light, local beer *(bia)* is available everywhere, and you could always try the rice wine. Mineral water *(nuoc suoi)* should never be drunk except from a sealed bottle. The fresh fruit juices are a delicious way to quench your thirst, but do not add ice cubes, which may be made from impure water.

A Basic Culinary Vocabulary

bread	*banh mi*
coconut milk	*nuoc dua*
coffee	*ca phe*
fish	*ca*
fruit	*trai cay*
meat	*thit*
milk	*sua*
noodles	*mi* or *bun*
rice	*com*
salt/pepper	*muoi/tieu*
stir-fried vegetables	*rau xao*
sugar	*duong*
tea	*nuoc tra*

SPORT AND ENTERTAINMENT

With 3,260 km (2,000 miles) of coastline, Vietnam is perfect for water sports, practised mainly around the areas of Ha Tien, Mui Ne and Nha Trang. Golf is developing, although it is still considered a rich man's game. Night-owls can experiment with karaoke or check out the local nightclubs.

Ball Games
Left to grow wild after the departure of the French, the country's golf courses are now being revived. Green fees can be extortionate, but they are gradually coming into line. There are courses at Ho Chi Minh City, Phan Tiet, Dalat, Hoi An, Danang and Hanoi. The Vietnamese are great fans of football and tennis, and also excel at badminton, volleyball and table tennis.

Water Sports
Dazzled by the cultural riches of the country and exhausted by sightseeing, you may fancy a few days of rest and relaxation by the sea. You'll not be disappointed, as many resorts can match coasts of Thailand, with fine sand, palm trees and warm water. Tourist development is in full swing, but some of the loveliest beaches are not yet equipped with facilities. Such is the pace of change, however, that things may quickly change.

The resort of Ha Tien, near the Cambodian border, is very popular. Vung Tau, near Ho Chi Minh City, attracts a lot of Vietnamese. At present Nha Trang and Mui Ne are the best-equipped. Surfing and windsurfing are slowly gaining in popularity. Diving is a bit disappointing, except off the Cham islands.

Other activities
Nightlife in Vietnamese cities is very much the same as you would find anywhere in the world. There are cinemas, theatres and nightclubs in all the large cities, and karaoke bars are all the rage.

The Vietnamese enjoy a legal flutter at the races, on slot machines and in lotteries: *mahjong* and cock-fighting are just as popular. The casinos are generally reserved for foreigners.

THE HARD FACTS

Here are some the practical details you will need to know when planning your trip to Vietnam.

Airports
Tan Son Nhat international airport is 7 km (4 miles) northwest of Ho Chi Minh City. Noi Bai international airport is 45 km (28 miles) north of Hanoi. Both airports handle direct flights per day from Europe or other Asian capitals. They both have money-changing facilities and information offices. Danang airport only serves other Asian cities. The new Long Thanh international airport, 40 km (25 miles) northeast of Ho Chi Minh City, will come into operation in 2020 and will almost totally replace Tan San Nhat for international flights.

Buses and taxis are available for transport to the city centres. An airport tax is charged on international flights from Ho Chi Minh City and Hanoi, and on some domestic flights.

Climate
The climate is not uniform from north to south. The best months are from October to April.

From December to February it can be cool and rainy in the north, average 13°C (55°F) but warm in the south, average 24°C (75°F). The monsoon affects everywhere except the centre from May to September, with temperatures reaching 35°C (95°F) in the south, and bright intervals between the downpours. Along the coast of the central region, the months of September to January are the wettest.

Communications
Post your letters in Hanoi or Ho Chi Minh City, from where they will take 2 or 3 weeks to reach Europe.

To make international calls, the easiest way is to go to the post office: you call from a cabin and pay afterwards at the cash desk. Rates are not expensive. You can also buy cards with an access code, or buy a SIM card from a local operator. If you take your own mobile phone, check that it is unblocked for international calls before you leave.

There are Internet cafés in large cities and some smaller towns. Most hotels have a computer with Internet access, sometimes free of charge.

Currency

The Vietnamese unit of currency is the Dong (VND). Banknotes are issued in denominations from 10,000 to 500,000 *dong*, coins from 200 to 5000. Old issue notes from 1000 to 5000 are also in circulation.

US dollars can be exchanged for *dong* in any bank or currency exchange office in large towns and touristic areas, but torn or damaged notes are not accepted. However, in most places you can pay directly in dollars. The major credit cards are accepted by some banks, luxury hotels, airlines, smart restaurants and the large travel agencies, but they charge a commission. If you use a credit card the amount will be noted in dollars unless you ask specifically for it to be in *dong*. ATMs dispense *dong* and charge a fee for each transaction.

Only travellers cheques in US$ can be converted into either dollars or *dong*; sterling or other cheques can be changed into *dong* only.

Customs

Visitors aged 18 or over are allowed to import duty-free 400 cigarettes, 100 cigars or 500 g tobacco; 1.5 litres alcoholic beverages over 22° or 2 litres under 22°, or 3 l other alcoholic drinks. Amounts of foreign currency imported exceeding US$5,000 or equivalent must be declared on arrival. You can export up to the same amount, but proof of expenses is required. Regulations change frequently so check with the Vietnamese embassy in your country prior to departure.

Electricity

In all the hotels, the supply is 220 volts AC, 50 Hz, though a few, rare places still have 110 volts. Plugs are European-type, with two round pins. Power cuts are still frequent in the south in the dry season (January to May).

Embassies and Consulates

Your embassy or consulate will be of help if you get into serious trouble, if you lose your passport, for example. Most countries are represented in Hanoi and Ho Chi Minh City.

Emergencies

Police 113, fire 114, ambulance 115.

Entry Formalities

Visas are required. A passport valid for at least six months after your date of arrival is necessary in order to obtain a visa. Your tour operator will take care of all the formalities on your behalf. Allow two weeks to a month for the documents to be prepared. It is possible to obtain a visa upon arrival at an airport in Vietnam;

the form can be filled in on-line, but you will need to obtain an approval letter from the immigration services (instructions are given on the consulate websites).

Make several photocopies of your passport, including visa, and keep them in different places, to avoid having to hand over the original whenever possible. You can also scan them and send them as an attachment in an e-mail addressed to yourself, so you can retrieve them wherever you are.

Essentials

Light cotton clothing is ideal for the south, with jeans and a sweater for the north. A light raincoat will be useful wherever you go. A pair of trainers, sandals and slip-ons for the evening are adequate as footwear. Carry a minimum of clothing as all city hotels have an efficient 24-hour laundry service. You can buy extra items on the spot. A hat, sunglasses, sunblock cream and insect repellent are vital. Take a pocket-lamp for when you visit caves or in case there is an electricity cut.

Health Precautions

No vaccinations are compulsory, but it is prudent to have valid poliomyelitis and tetanus protection. Vaccination against hepatitis B is strongly recommended. Depending on the area you are visiting, a preventive treatment against malaria should also be taken, according to your doctor's or chemist's recommendations.

Your basic supplies should include medication for intestinal problems, travel sickness and allergic reactions (insect bites). If you have a regular prescription medecine, then take it with you just to be safe.

In recent years, Vietnam has greatly improved its food hygiene standards. Nevertheless, it is only sensible to observe a few basic rules: never eat raw vegetables or fruit that you have not personally peeled. Stick to bottled water and, whenever possible, drink and brush your teeth with mineral water too (and make sure the seal is intact). You can buy purification tablets to add to boiled water before you leave. Fresh fruit juice is excellent, but avoid the ice cubes. Milk should also be boiled, or reconstituted using pure water.

Languages

Vietnamese is the language of the vast majority. English is most commonly spoken in the south (partly as a legacy of the American presence, but also reflecting growing trade, tourism and educational influences). A knowledge of French survives among the declining number of old people who experienced the French colonial era.

Opening Hours
These are not likely to be a problem as the Vietnamese seem to work non-stop!

State-run shops, banks and offices generally open Monday to Friday 7.30 or 8–11.30 a.m. and 1–4 p.m. Private shops open 8 or 8.30 a.m. to 9 or 10 p.m. Street traders stay open as long as there are clients to buy their wares.

Post offices open every day, including holidays, 6 or 7 a.m.–8 p.m. (later in big cities).

Photography
Remember to take a good supply of memory cards for your digital camera, and don't forget your battery charger.

It is forbidden to photograph military installations. If you want to take pictures of the ethnic minorities, it is best to ask their permission beforehand.

Public Holidays
These are the nine official public holidays, when people get the day off work.

Jan 1	New Year
Jan–Feb	Tet (New Year) (last day of last lunar month to 3rd day of first lunar month)
April	Hung Kings Temple Festival (10th day of 3rd lunar month)
Apr 30	Liberation of Saigon, Reunification
May 1	Labour Day
Sept 2	National Day

Among the other holidays are

Feb 3	Foundation of Vietnamese Communist Party
May 19	Ho Chi Minh's Birthday
June 28	Family Day
July 27	Remembrance Day
Aug 9	Revolution Commemoration Day
Oct 10	Capital Liberation Day
Oct 20	Women's Day
Nov 20	Teachers' Day
Dec 22	National Defense Day
Dec 25	Christmas Day

There are also several lunar holidays such as Buddha's Birthday, the Lantern Festival and the Ghost Festival.

Security
Even in the big cities, there is not much crime in Vietnam, but petty theft is common. Keep an eye open for pickpockets in crowded places and avoid any display of wealth. It is better to leave your jewellery, money and important documents (passport, airline ticket) in the hotel safe.

Social Customs
Shoes are removed before entering religious sanctuaries and dwellings. In general, women should avoid being too skimpily clad in the temples and forego

topless bathing on the beach. Bikinis are not a problem, but may encourage unwelcome attention. Small problems are best resolved with a smile. It is a pointless exercise to show displeasure or impatience. You will be better served by explaining calmly but firmly the reasons for your complaint without losing your sense of humour. Vietnamese are conciliatory and civilized. Their main fault is that they don't want to lose face, so they may answer "Yes" to your questions even if they haven't understood. So it's best to avoid questions that require yes or no for an answer.

Time Difference
Vietnam operates at UTC/GMT + 7, which means seven hours ahead of UK in winter and six hours ahead in summer.

Tipping
Service charges in large hotels and restaurants are generally included in the bill. If you stay more than one night in a hotel, you could leave a little extra for the chambermaid. In smaller restaurants and bars, a tip for good service is always appreciated, and baggage porters expect a tip. If you use the services of a driver or a guide, give them the equivalent of at least US$1 per day.

Transport
There are regular flights from Ho Chi Minh City, Danang and Hanoi to all the principal towns of Vietnam. It is advisable to reserve flights several days in advance, especially during the New Year festivities. You can book flights on the Internet.

Vietnam has a railway network running mainly along the coast from Ho Chi Minh City to Hanoi (a two-day journey) and Haiphong. There are several classes, ranging from the soft couchette to the very economical hard seat. For information, see the website of Vietnam railways: vietnam-railway.com. It's more comfortable and easier to book with open tour private companies.

Individual travellers may find that a private car with driver is the most practical way of getting around: this way you can stop whenever you wish. Non residents are not allowed to drive.

In town, the cycle-rickshaw (*cyclo*) is by far the best method of transport: agree on the price before you set out. Vinasun and Mai Linh taxi companies are reliable and have a very good reputation. Mototaxis are a cheaper possibility but don't have as much charm, and given the increased number of road accidents, are probably best avoided. It's more complicated to use the bus network.

INDEX

An Binh 61
Ba Be, National Park 28
Bac Lieu 59
Bai Chay 26
Ban Don 41
Binh Hoa Phuoc 61
Ca Mau 59
Cai Be 61–63
Can Tho 58
Cao Bang 28
Cat Ba 26
Cau Da 43–44
Champa Kingdom 44
Cham temples 44–45
Chau Doc 57
Cholon 51–52
Chua But Thap 23–24
Chua Huong 22–23
Chua Thay 23
Chua Tay Phuong 23
Cu Chi Tunnels 52–53
Cua Lo 32
Dalat 45–46
Danang 37–39
Demilitarized zone 32–33
Dien Bien Phu 29
Do Son 25
Ferry Road 25
Ha Long Bay 26–27
Ha Tien 59
Haiphong 25
Hang Pac Bo 28
Hanoi 17–22
   Chua Mot Cot 19
   Den Hai Ba Trung 21
   Den Quan Than
   Ho Chi Mausoleum 19–20
   Ho Hoan Kiem 17–18
   Hoa Lo Prison 21
   Imperial City 59
   Museums:
   – Hanoi 21
   – Military 21
   – of Revolution 21
   Vietnam Ethnology 21–22
   Vietnamese History 21
   Presidential Palace 20
   Tran Quoc 59
   Van Mieu 18–19
   Vielle Ville 59
Hien Luong Bridge 32
Hoa Binh 24
Hoa Lu 24–25
Hoang Son 32
Ho Chi Minh City 49–51
Ho Chi Minh Trail 33
Hoi An 39–40
Hon Chong 43
Hon Mieu 43
Hon Mun 43
Hon Yen 43–44
Hué 33–37
Inland Route 41
Kim Lien 32
Lam Son 31
Lang Co 37
Lang Son 28
Long Hai 54
Mandarin Road 31
Marble Mountains 38–39
Mekong Delta 54–63,
   fold-out map
Meo Zao 27
My Son 40
My Tho 63
Mui Ne 47
Nha Trang 41–44
Oc-Eo 59
Perfume Pagoda
   see Chua Huong
Phan Thiet 47
Phong Nha 32
Phong Nha-Ke Bang NP 32
Po Klong Garai 44–45
Po Rome 45
Rach Gia 59
Red River 23
Sa Dec 60
Sa Pa 28–29
Saigon see Ho Chi Minh City
Sam, Mount 57
Soc Trang 59
Song Hong 23
Tam Coc 24–25
Tan Chau 57
Tay Ninh 53
Thanh Hoa 31
Tram Chim NP 60
Truong Son, cemetery 32
Vinh 31–32
Vinh Long 60–61
Vinh Moc Tunnels 33
Vinh Xuong 54
Vung Tau 54
Water puppets 20
Waterfall Road 46–47
Xeo Quyt 60
Yok Don National Park 41

Editor
Petronella Greenhalgh

Revisions
Theresa Lachner

Design
Karin Palazzolo

Layout
Luc Malherbe
Matias Jolliet

Photo credits
p. 1 istockphoto.com/Videowok_Art
p. 2 istockphoto.com/Serdar Yagci (birdcage); istockphoto.com/Molloykeith (bicycle); hemis.fr/Maisant (bonsai); Renata Holzbachová (dragon)

Maps
JPM Publications,
Mathieu Germay

Copyright © 2013, 1999
JPM Publications S.A.
12, avenue William-Fraisse,
1006 Lausanne, Suisse
information@jpmguides.com
http://www.jpmguides.com/

All rights reserved. No part of this publication may be reproduced or transmitted in any form or by any means, electronic or mechanical, including photocopying, recording or by any information storage and retrieval system without permission in writing from the publisher.

Every care has been taken to verify the information in the guide, but the publisher cannot accept responsibility for any errors that may have occurred. If you spot an inaccuracy or a serious omission, please let us know.

Printed in Switzerland
15166.00.15289
Edition 2014

CRUISING THE MEKONG

It is impossible to overstate the importance of the Mekong and the vast web of its delta in the life of the people who live along its banks. Everything from the history and politics of the region to its culture and cuisine is built on the mighty river and its tributaries. The best way to see it is by boat, soaking up the fascination of one of the world's greatest waterways.

As early as 7000 BC, the rich waterlands of the Mekong and its delta provided the means for rice production and other forms of agriculture. Still today, the delta is the rice-basket of Vietnam, while fish farms provide a living for the Cambodians along the banks of the Tonle Sap, designated a UNESCO biosphere in 1997. On a cruise, you'll witness all the glories of a timeless landscape and its ancient past. Sampans and speedboats share the river. The cone-hatted fisherman checking his wicker traps will probably be touting a mobile phone in his back pocket, while the great towns—Vientiane, Phnom Penh, Ho Chi Minh City—are immersed in the full-blooded modernity of high-tech commercialism, while the Upper Mekong nations plan to build more hydroelectric dams.

Going with the Flow

From the border between Thailand and Laos, the Mekong winds sinuously through forests, whose trees trail long tendrils in the water, and through areas of steep limestone cliffs. To the north can be seen distant green mountains, still home to remote animist tribal people such as the Hmong, Mien and Akha.

Upriver from the ancient royal capital of Luang Prabang, the fascinating **Pak Ou Caves** have become a sanctuary for old or damaged images of the Buddha from the city's temples. A gentle 25-km meander along the Mekong brings a first sighting of the golden-spired stupa on top of the "holy hill" at the centre of **Luang Prabang**. This charming city retains its place at the heart of Lao culture: with its palaces and temples, and early-morning parade of saffron-robed monks, it's the most gently seductive city in South-East Asia.

From here the Mekong descends south to Laos's bustling capital, **Vientiane**, founded in the 16th century on a wide bend in the river, but laid out by French colonialists around a century ago.

Around 20 km east of Vientiane is the 1170-m **First Friendship Bridge**. When it opened in 1994 it was the first crossing point into Thailand. Traffic on the bridge drives on the left, as in Thailand, and changes over to the right at the Laos end. The river here supports thousands of fishing and farming communities, whose members live in thatched stilt huts raised above the water.

The largest town in southern Laos is **Pakse**, nestling at the confluence of the Mekong and the Xe Don, with Laos's second bridge across the river, built with Japanese aid in 2000. This cosmopolitan town is the gateway to the coffee and tea plantations of the **Bolovens Plateau**, as well as the riverside village of **Ban Saphay**, known for its tradition of cloth weaving on hand looms. On the right bank of the river, just south of Pakse, are the ancient **Khmer ruins** of Wat Phou and on the left, those of Um Muang.

The river has one last surprise in Laos before flowing into Cambodia—the **Khon Phapheng** falls are the biggest in South-East Asia, best seen in the dry season from March to May before the water level rises too high.

Around 150 km beyond the Cambodian border, **Kratie** is an attractive if sleepy riverside town, famous for its small colony of freshwater dolphins, rare aquatic mammals now endangered as the river silts up. Downstream from Kratie, the hilltop temple of **Wat Hanchey** commands a superb view of the Mekong. The ancient brick structure has survived from the 8th-century Chenla dynasty which ruled this region for two centuries before the ascendancy of Angkor, but is surrounded by modern buildings.

Nearby **Kampong Cham** is worth stopping off at for its small collection of fine colonial era buildings, lively waterfront district and, in the vicinity, the 12th-century sandstone and laterite **Wat Nokor** enclosing a modern Theravda Buddhist pagoda. Kampong Cham is also an important crossroads for anyone contemplating a visit to **Angkor**. A relatively good main road runs from here to Siem Reap (200 km). If you take the land route rather than continuing along the Mekong, be sure to make a detour to see the market at **Skuon** village, where you can snack a local delicacy, fried spider (they are specially bred in holes in the ground).

If you decide to go all the way to Angkor by boat, you will stay on the Mekong to the Cambodian capital, **Phnom Penh** at the confluence with the **Tonlé Sap River**, and travel north from there.

Some 15 km upstream from **Udong** on the Tonle Sap, **Kampong Tralach** is a small village set amid rice paddies. A stroll inland brings you to the small and isolated Wat Kampong Tralach Leu pagoda. Further upstream you come to **Kampong Chhnang**, a town in the province of the same name, with a busy fish trade.

The Tonle Sap flows out of the vast waters of the 100-km-long **Tonle Sap Lake** to the north of which is **Siem Reap**, an affluent tourist town, close to the Angkor temples.

Below Phnom Penh, the mighty Mekong is reaching the end of its long journey through South-East Asia. The river starts to break up and, as it enters Vietnam, widens into the delta, eventually emptying into the South China Sea. On one of the river's

branches is the vibrant **Ho Chi Minh City**, which the Vietnamese still call Saigon. On the way there you might stop off at **Tan Chau**, where most visitors hop onto a trishaw, xe loi, to look around family-run silk-weaving factories. A substance from the ebony tree, Diospyros mollis, is used to dye the silk black. You can also cruise the canals on small boats, passing beneath fragile-looking "monkey bridges".

The rapidly expanding city of **Can Tho**, with a population of over a million, makes an excellent base for visiting many of the delta's attractions. It has plenty of hotels, and the people are renowned for their hospitality.

The industrial and commercial port of **Sa Dec** was the site of an American Swift Boat base during the Vietnam War. It was here that in 1929 the French writer Marguerite Duras (1914–96) become involved with the 27-year-old son of a wealthy Chinese family, the subject of her prize-winning novel The Lover. At the time Duras was 15 years old.

Near the city of **Vinh Long**, a lively provincial capital set between two branches of the Mekong, **Cai Be** is a small river port with an interesting floating market, busiest in the early morning. Visitors get the chance to step aboard houseboats and chat with members of the family, as well as seeing cottage industries such as coconut candy or puffed rice workshops, ricepaper-making and visiting local potters, brickworks and orchards.

Head south, and the urban sprawl gives way to a network of channels containing floating villages, fish farms, fruit plantations and rice paddies. This rich, watery area is one of the most productive food-growing areas in South-East Asia.

You'll find detailed information about all the stopovers in the respective guides.

CAMBODIA

Dan Colwell

CONTENTS

83	This Way Cambodia
87	Flashback
93	On the Scene
93	Phnom Penh
101	The Mekong
105	Tonle Sap Waterway
111	The Angkor Sites
117	West Cambodia
119	Shopping
120	Dining Out
122	The Hard Facts
128	Index

Maps
102 Kratie
108 Siem Reap

Fold-out map
Cambodia
Phnom Penh
Angkor Temples

Buddhist beliefs

grandiose monuments

life on the waterways

fragrant offerings

THIS WAY CAMBODIA

Mention the word Cambodia, and it immediately conjures up idyllic images of intricate monumental art, graceful traditional dancers and peasants hoeing in rice fields or plowing with water buffaloes—but also nightmares of cruelty and suffering, and the ruthless destruction of a proud cultural heritage.

Who could have imagined back in the 1960s the disastrous path Cambodia was about to embark upon? At that time, the kingdom of Cambodia, also called Srok Khmer, Land of the Khmers, was inhabited by a healthy, essentially rural population. Having recently emerged from French colonial rule, the people appeared to live a tranquil and pacific life under the leadership of Prince Sihanouk, who was nudging the country forward towards the modern world.

But after 1970, the kingdom was thrown into chaos: first came the deposition of the prince and the declaration of a republic. Then Cambodia felt the full, terrible effect of the Vietnam War (1970–75). This was followed by the ordeal of four years under the totalitarian Khmer Rouge regime headed by the infamous Pol Pot, when the people were transformed into slaves of the state and the cultural patrimony of the nation systematically eradicated. There was no escaping this madness—which resulted in the deaths of millions of citizens by massacre, starvation and disease—except by paying the price of foreign occupation. In 1979, disaffected Khmer troops backed by the Vietnamese Army invaded Cambodia and overthrew the Pol Pot government.

A Hopeful Future

Little by little, Cambodia has striven to heal its wounds and to open the door to the future. In the last few years the reconstruction of the nation's political, economic and cultural life has gathered pace. For a start, the monarchy—the symbolic and aesthetic core of its equilibrium—has been restored. Parts of Cambodia such as the areas north and west of Siem Reap, which were closed off until the late 1990s due to the threat of

Graceful in its gestures, Khmer dancing is associated with the Royal Court.

banditry by remnants of the Khmer Rouge, are now open for travel. A fast, comfortable highway has been built to link Phnom Penh with the coastal resort of Sihanoukville. The road connecting the capital to Siem Reap and the temples at Angkor was also greatly improved. Several resorts and facilities from the Colonial era are being brought back to life along the coast, as at Sihanoukville and Kep (Krong Keb). Established as getaways for French civil servants in the early 20th century who called it Kep-sur-Mer, the long-abandoned estates and villas are now enjoying a renaissance as boutique hotels.

Many international companies are based in Phnom Penh, and yet it remains a quiet city with large avenues, enlivened by a typically Southeast Asian dynamism. Tourists are filled with wonder at the temples of Angkor, among the world's greatest sights. The nearby town of Siem Reap is undergoing a boom, with a flurry of hotel-building taking place.

Carnival on Water

Demonstrating a welcome continuity with the past, the lives of the 15 million inhabitants, over 90 per cent of whom are ethnic Khmer, remain closely tied to the ebb and flow of the Mekong River. The capital, Phnom Penh, rises at the junction of the Mekong and one of its tributaries, the Tonle Sap, whose waters feed into a small lake on the north side of town. This tributary is unusual in that it reverses its flow twice a year. From October to June, it flows from the northwest to the southeast, but at the beginning of June, the pressure of the Mekong, then starting to flood, is so great that it manages to push back the Tonle Sap, causing it to run upstream and spill into the great lake of the same name in the centre of the country, thus increasing its depth five-fold. The seasonal reversal of the waters in late October is the occasion of a grand spectacle in Phnom Penh, the Water Festival, featuring colourful canoe races. In the old days, the king would order a royal monk to cut a rope stretched across the river, thus "liberating" the waters and reversing the current. Modern Cambodians use it as an excuse to pour into the capital and celebrate the sheer marvel of the nation's survival.

Few could claim that travel here is easy—many secondary roads have more potholes than flat surfaces, and facilities outside the main cities often leave a lot to be desired. But wherever you go in Cambodia, your way will be smoothed along by its fascinating landscape, the grandeur of its monuments and the charm and friendliness of its people.

The gigantic carved heads of Angkor Thom's Bayon face the four points of the compass.

FLASHBACK

The first settlements in Cambodia date back to around 4000 BC. Around 3000 BC, Neolithic peoples from southern China migrated to the Indochinese peninsula. Archaeological evidence suggests they lived in houses built on wooden piles and ate mainly fish, practices strikingly similar to those of rural Cambodians today.

From the 1st century, the culture took on a decided Indian cast, mainly due to the establishment of trade links between South-East Asia and the sub-continent. Indeed, Hinduism would exist alongside Buddhism as a central aspect of Khmer culture for the next thousand years.

By the 3rd century a Sanskrit-style alphabet was in place, along with Indian-influenced arts and religion. At this time a Hindu-Buddhist kingdom ruled Cambodia and southern Vietnam; the Chinese—the only source of information on the period—knew it as Funan. From the Mekong delta, the kingdom became a powerful maritime empire and expanded over most of the Indochinese peninsula.

Funan began to decline during the 6th century. Chinese writers refer to two successor kingdoms in the region: Water Chenla, which occupied the delta, and Land Chenla, based further up the Mekong in northern Cambodia and southern Laos. Over the next three centuries, these seem to have fragmented even further into several small kingdoms. Politically divided, the region became prey to attacks from the expansionist Buddhist Srivijaya empire. Yet from this dangerously vulnerable position, Khmer culture was about to enter its golden age.

Angkor Period

In 790 a young prince from Java, who claimed Cambodian descent, gained a foothold in the eastern part of the country. By 802 he had established his capital in the north of Cambodia, not far from where Angkor was later built, and was consecrated as a *chakravatin* (an Indian concept of "world ruler") under the name of Jayavarman II. Vital in creating a unified, centralized state, his reign ushered in the long and glorious era of

classical Khmer civilization. Soon after his death, the capital was moved to Roluos, just north of the Tonle Sap lake. Here, his successor Indravarman I built the first of the great Khmer monuments, including the Bakong, a temple-mountain which served as a model for many of the subsequent royal temples at Angkor.

Indravarman's son, Yasovarman I (reigned 889–910), shifted the capital to Angkor itself. Buddhism began to spread throughout the region, complementing Hinduism. Relying on an agrarian economy with increasingly sophisticated methods of irrigation, Angkor developed into the foremost regional power, taking control of the Mekong Valley and central Vietnam, and pushing its empire into present-day Laos and Thailand. Several of its rulers used the wealth and manpower of the nation to build magnificent palaces and temples. However, the draining effect this had on the society was partly responsible for some of its subsequent difficulties. Angkor was subject to periodic bouts of disorder and war-

Ancient Khmer script on a stone tablet at Angkor. | ***Râmakerti*** **wall painting in the Silver Pagoda of Phnom Penh's Royal Palace.** | **Colonial relic in Phnom Penh.** | **A basketful of baguettes, introduced by the French.**

fare during the 10th and 11th centuries, and faced disintegration as rival contenders fought for the throne.

Nonetheless, the rise of a new dynasty in the 12th century marked the apogee of Khmer culture. With the accession of Suryavarman II in 1113, Angkor once again had a mighty warrior-king on the throne. He led a celebrated campaign against the Champa kingdom of Vietnam but is best known today as the builder of Angkor Wat. There was one more great king to come. In 1177 Jayavarman VII repelled the Chams after they had sacked Angkor. To further protect the state he had the huge city of Angkor Thom constructed, with the extraordinary Bayon temple at its centre. But the state had already begun to pass its peak. At the death of Jayavarman VII, in around 1219, Angkor had reached the beginning of the end.

Fall of Angkor

The decline turned out to be long and gradual. But eventually the arrival of more dynamic Indochinese empires, coupled with a transformation in the structure of the state—the hierarchical Hindu concept of god-king was replaced by Theravada Buddhism—took their toll. Repeated attacks on Angkor in the 14th and 15th centuries by the Thai kingdom based at Ayutthaya devastated Khmer power. The city was sacked in 1351, then again in 1431, after which Angkor was abandoned and the new capital of Phnom Penh, Lovek, founded at the confluence of the Mekong and the Tonle Sap river. Apart from a brief resurgence in the mid-16th century, the Khmers underwent a series of weak monarchs and bad defeats, becoming a vassal state of their neighbours.

In 1794 the Thais appropriated Angkor and the western provinces of Cambodia. To the east, the Vietnamese seized the Mekong delta and the Khmer port of Prey Nokor, the future Saigon. Gradually, the whole region was systematically Vietnamized.

French Rule

During the 19th century Cambodia's kings relied more and more on foreign support, in effect becoming pawns in a power struggle between the Thais and Vietnamese. By the middle of the century the country was facing the threat of being completely swallowed up by its neighbours, and so King Norodom signed a treaty with France in 1863 turning Cambodia into a French protectorate. King Nomrod managed to control the country's internal politics until his death in 1904, after which the French were able to further impose their will.

Meanwhile, French archaeologists began excavations at Angkor, bringing it to the attention of the outside world. In 1907 it was finally returned to Cambodian control by the Thais.

Under pressure from the Japanese, Vichy France appointed the 18-year-old Prince Sihanouk to the throne in 1941. During World War II, Thailand seized western Cambodia, including Angkor, and Japan took control of the rest. France regained power in 1945, but eight years later Cambodia achieved independence. Sihanouk had been instrumental in the negotiations with the French, and in 1954 his government was recognized as the legitimate authority in the nation.

Cambodia and the Vietnam War

Though Sihanouk followed a policy of neutrality in relation to the war raging in Vietnam, his suspicion of American intentions in the region meant that he was broadly sympathetic to the North Vietnamese communists. As a result, in 1970 the pro-American General Lon Nol overthrew Sihanouk and launched an attack on North Vietnamese troops stationed inside the eastern border of the country. This proved a disastrous move on two counts. The Cambodian army, no match for the battle-hardened Vietnamese, was easily defeated, and it had the effect of involving Cambodia in the Vietnam War. Even worse, when the Vietnam War officially ended after the Paris cease-fire agreement in 1973, the Cambodian communists (the Khmer Rouge) refused to adhere to it. In response, the Americans carried out massive aerial bombardments of Cambodia, despite there being no state of war between the countries. In fact, the US dropped more bombs on the country than it had on Japan during the whole of World War II. Paradoxically, the main result of the havoc wreaked by this was to hasten the collapse of the Lon Nol government. In April 1975, Khmer Rouge troops entered Phnom Penh, opening a new and terrible chapter of Cambodian history.

Khmer Rouge in Power

Under the leadership of Saloth Sar, a former teacher better known as Pol Pot, and influenced by the Cultural Revolution in Mao's China, the Khmer Rouge set about establishing a totally collectivized state, where the entire population was forced to work the land in the effort to increase rice production. Phnom Penh and other towns were emptied; people suspected of being from the educated middle class were systematically murdered, while many more died from overwork, starvation and disease. The country was effectively cut off from the rest of the world for the next four years.

In 1979, the regime's belligerence towards Vietnam prompted a military invasion that swept aside the army and caused the Khmer Rouge leadership to flee to Thailand. During their short time in power, the Khmer Rouge had been responsible for the deaths of at least 1.5 million Cambodians—a quarter of the total population.

Cambodia Today

Under the political influence of Vietnam, Cambodia returned to something approaching normality. Private property was re-introduced, the practice of Buddhism permitted and the art of traditional dance revived; schools were reopened and the cities repopulated. When the Vietnamese withdrew in 1989, the country was still left to face considerable problems, not least from continuing Khmer Rouge guerrilla activity in the north and west. And though Sihanouk was restored to the throne in 1993, the political scene remained extremely volatile. The 1997 elections saw one of his sons, royalist Prince Ranariddh, elected as prime minister, only to be ousted in a coup led by his co-incumbent, pro-Vietnam Hun Sen. New elections in 1998—the same year that Pol Pot died in the jungle out on the Thai border—placed Hun Sen's Cambodian People's Party in power. Re-elected in 2008, Hun Sen is still Prime Minister.

King Sihanouk abdicated in 2004, several years before his death in 2012, and was succeeded by another of his sons, who took the name Norodom Sihamoni. Born in 1953, he had been a ballet dancer and also Cambodia's ambassador to UNESCO, and had stayed out of politics. Cambodia has a rediscovered pride in its cultural heritage and optimism about the future.

Victims of the Pol Pot regime are commemorated in the Toul Sleng Genocide Museum.

Moto-taxis are a common form of public transport in Phnom Penh.

ON THE SCENE

Cambodia has two main hubs. Phnom Penh, the capital, provides a perfect introduction to the culture, with its Royal Palace and museums. From the centre, speedboats head northeast to Kratie, where there's a group of rare Irrawaddy dolphins, while buses run to the laid-back beach resort of Sihanoukville, basking by the warm waters of the Gulf of Thailand. Almost every visitor will stay in Siem Reap at some point. This pleasant, burgeoning little town is the base for trips to Cambodia's world renowned temples at Angkor. From here you will also find boats that go into the northwest of the country, where out-of-the-way towns such as Battambang retain their attractive colonial-era architecture.

Phnom Penh

With its bustling boulevards and markets, riverside walks and fascinating mix of modern and traditional buildings, Phnom Penh has an unmistakable charm. It was founded in 1434 once the Khmers had left Angkor but was abandoned between 1505 and 1865, when King Norodom established it as his capital under the French Protectorate. During this period, the Royal Palace, National Museum and several colonial buildings were erected. Once known as the "Pearl of Asia", the city was occupied by the Japanese in WW II, and in 1975 the entire population was evacuated by the Khmer Rouge. Throughout the city's traumatic recent history, the Royal Palace quarter remained the symbolic heart of the nation, and is the obvious place to begin your visit.

Palace Quarter

Ranged around the Royal Palace are monasteries, ministries, workshops and residences, forming respectively the monarchy's four pillars of religion, politics, art and family. Most of the buildings here date from the era of French rule, and as you wander around the leafy streets of the quarter it's possible to see in their scale and grandeur a reflection of colonial, rather than royal, power.

Royal Palace

Located behind a protective wall topped with lotus-shaped crenellations, the Royal Palace has once more become the residence of the king. It's composed of a number of large and small pavilions set in courtyards according to a specific layout, where material objects oppose things spiritual, and public faces private. At the end of the 19th century, the palace was a small city in itself with several thousand people bustling about. The majority of the buildings were pulled down for reconstruction in the 1910s.

Bestriding the wall, and facing the river, the **Chan Chaya Pavilion** was originally the impressive entrance to the palace and used for special performances of Khmer music and dance.

The **Throne Hall** is behind the pavilion. Despite its modern appearance (it was rebuilt in 1917), it's one of the most beautiful examples of Cambodian architecture, and deeply influenced by classical Khmer style. The splendid spire is adorned with a four-faced head of Brahmâ. The sumptuous interior, visible from the outside (access and photos are strictly forbidden), is covered with murals depicting scenes from *Râmakerti*, the Cambodian version of the *Ramayana*.

Not far from here is the weirdly anomalous **Napoleon Pavilion**, given by Napoleon III to the Empress Eugénie and then passed on as a gift to King Norodom in 1876. The building, with its cast-iron pillars, is being renovated.

Reached via a gate just south of the pavilion, the **Silver Pagoda** was built from wood in 1892, then reconstructed in 1962. It's so named because the floor is paved with more than 5,000 silver tiles weighing a kilogram apiece. The pagoda shelters a superb standing golden Buddha, adorned with 9584 diamonds, the collective work of several jewellers at the beginning of the 20th century. At the back is a small, exquisite seated Emerald Buddha dating from the 17th century, which is in fact made of crystal. On the walls of the outside courtyard is a fine set of traditional paintings illustrating the *Râmakerti*.

The complex includes the pagoda, royal stupas, libraries, a pavilion containing a footprint of the Buddha, and an equestrian statue of King Norodom.

National Museum

Just north of the palace, the National Museum was built in pure Khmer style in 1917 by a French architect, with the help of the last traditional local architects. It houses a first-rate collection of Khmer art dating from the pre-Angkorian era through to the 20th century.

The principal highlights of the museum are the sculptures, statues, stelae, bronzes and other artefacts retrieved from Angkor, notably the red sandstone bas-relief from Banteay Srei and the sublime portrait head of Jayavarman VII, dating from the late 12th century. Throughout the country you'll see recreations of this image representing one of Angkor's greatest kings.

Sisowath Quay

Running north from the Royal Palace along the Tonle Sap river, Sisowath Quay is lined with cafés and restaurants and is a constant hive of activity. You'll find early-morning joggers, late-afternoon strollers and at all times a bevy of fruit sellers and drink stalls. All of Phnom Penh gathers each afternoon to enjoy the sunset. There's a good night market on Friday, Saturday and Sunday evenings. The views

A praying Buddha intricately worked in iron, on the gates of the the Royal Palace, shows the exquisite attention to detail. | **The National Museum, built in an interpretation of the traditional Khmer temple style.**

Stunning decor at Wat Phnom, where worshippers flock to pray for good fortune.

reach across to where the Tonle Sap meets the Mekong. You can also take boats from here out onto the river.

Wat Ounalom

Set back from the Tonle Sap to the north of the National Museum, this large temple complex is the headquarters of Cambodian Buddhism. It was founded in the 15th century, soon after the Khmers left Angkor. The temple's prominence in the religious life of the country meant that in the late 1970s it became the focus of Khmer Rouge aggression, when its chief priest was murdered and the important library of Buddhist texts destroyed.

Other attractions

The distances covered in this section might be too great to accomplish entirely on foot, especially in very hot weather. The best solution is to catch a tuk-tuk or to hop on the back of a *moto* to get from one place to another—the drivers are generally very good, and it's an entertaining way to see the city.

Independence Monument

This huge monument occupies a traffic island south of the Palace Quarter at the corner of Norodom and Sihanouk boulevards. Built in the shape of a lotus and adorned with 100 nagas—mythical, multi-headed snakes—it was completed in 1958 and celebrates Cambodia's independence from France, which took place five years earlier.

Central Market

Away from the river, the busy streets in the centre of town converge on the yellow ochre façade of the huge Psar Thmei (Central Market). Built in Art Deco style by the French in 1937, with four wings radiating from the central dome, it houses a marvellous range of stalls selling everything from jewellery to toasted spiders, and should be visited by anyone wanting colourful photos of Cambodian life.

Wat Phnom

To the north of the city centre, Wat Phnom is situated on a hill 27 m high ("Phnom" means hill in Khmer). Legend has it that in 1372, a nun named Penh discovered four statues of the Buddha on the nearby riverbank and placed them in a purpose-built pagoda on the hill. The settlement that grew up around it acquired the name Phnom Penh, the hill of Penh. There's a small statue of Lady Penh in the pavilion next to the large stupa containing the ashes of King Ponhea Yat, who died in 1467 and was the Angkorian king responsible for establishing Phnom Penh as the nation's main city after the abandonment of Angkor.

The temple can be reached via a superb staircase guarded by terracotta lions and two nagas.

Colonial Quarter

The former French end of town stretches around Wat Phnom and continues northwards. Here there remain fine colonial houses, the administrative offices of the old protectorate (including various public buildings in colonial style), the Lycée français René Descartes, the Calmette Hospital and the French Embassy, both on Monivong Boulevard, and the Bibliothèque Nationale. This is next to the famous Hotel Le Royal, which opened in 1929. Following years of neglect after the rise of the Khmer Rouge, it has now been restored to its former splendour.

South of the City

The area south of central Phnom Penh is home to the well-known Psar Toul Tom Poung or **Russian Market**, named after the migrants who frequented it in the 1980s. It attracts many visitors to its food stalls and shops which sell a variety of fabrics, clothing, crafts, jewellery and other souvenirs.

Toul Sleng Museum

Located in the former Toul Svay Prey High School only a kilometre or so from the city centre, this is also known as the Genocide Museum. It's never less than a grim experience, but perhaps also a vital one for any understanding of modern Cambodian history. During the Khmer Rouge regime, the school was run by a secret department code-named S-21; it served as a centre of interrogation and torture for people of all ages and social ranks. Almost unbearably harrowing photographs, paintings, eye-witness accounts and other documents testify to the murderous insanity that gripped the country's leadership and its functionaries at the time, and the terrible price that its citizens had to pay.

Killing Fields of Choeung Ek

The victims of Toul Sleng's torture cells were brought to these fields 15 km (9 miles) south of the city, where they were usually bludgeoned to death to avoid the cost of using bullets. After the Pol Pot regime was defeated by the Vietnamese army in 1979, the mass graves found here contained the remains of thousands of people (an estimated 20,000). It's now a peaceful, solemn place, and the memorial stupa filled with the skulls of those found nearby makes an emotive centrepiece. All around are the craters from which the bodies were exhumed.

Tonle Bati

This lake lies 33 km (20 miles) south of Phnom Penh. The area is a popular haunt of weekend day trippers, who come to cool off by the river or float on one of the swan-shaped pleasure boats. There are several interesting sites, including the remains of a couple of Angkor-era cities.

On the lake shore, the temple of **Ta Prohm** was built in the 12th century by Jayavarman VII. Made from laterite, decorated with bas-reliefs and sculptures, and with a layout similar to Angkor's grand temples, it gives a good idea of the essence of classical Khmer architecture if you are unable to get to Angkor itself. Be sure also to visit the nearby, smaller **Yeay Peau** temple.

A further 20 km (12 miles) to the south are the 11th-century hilltop ruins of **Phnom Chisor**. The main temple, dedicated to Brahma, took a pounding from Lon Nol's troops and bombers in the early 1970s but still has some fine features, such as the carved sandstone lintels. Further compensation comes from the spectacular views of the countryside and the Tonle Om lake.

Colonial memories. | From the age of six, girls can start training for the Apsara dance at the Khmer Dance School.

A bewitching palette of pinks and yellows in the sunset at Kratie.

The Mekong

Just south of Phnom Penh the Mekong is coming to the end of its 4,350-km (2,700-mile) journey down from the Tibetan plateau, before it enters Vietnam 60 km (37 miles) further south and breaks up into the multiple arms of the delta. The stretch between Phnom Penh and Kratie is served by leisurely cruises that will give you the impression that somehow you have drifted from the bustling present into the Southeast Asia of ancient memory, as the river traffic laden with commercial and industrial goods gives way to the rural bliss and green forests of the Cambodian countryside.

You can also travel by road from Phnom Penh to Kratie, but in places it is the stuff of nightmares. Far better to go the longer and calmer route by booking a boat trip with two or three nights on board (not in the dry season), soaking up the fascination of life along one of the world's greatest river systems. It is impossible to overstate the importance of the Mekong to the Cambodian people. As you sail along, stopping off to visit floating villages and larger towns with museums and ancient temples, you will be continually aware that, like the traditional stilt houses dotted along its banks, everything from the history and politics of the region to its culture and cuisine is built on the river and its tributaries.

Koh Dach

Just 15 km (9 miles) north of Phnom Penh, this large river island with its stilt villages and fine sandy beach (also called Koh Dait) is a pleasure ground for day trippers, who can board boats near Wat Ounalom. Once on the island you can ride on an elephant, see silk being woven and enjoy classical Khmer dancing. The residents are mainly boat fishermen—look out for the unusual boat temple.

Koh Chen

Further north is the floating village of Koh Chen (literally, Chinese Island). Its inhabitants practice their copper and silver crafts, and you can watch them at work in their open workshops. Jewellery and silverware are beautifully engraved.

Koh Paen

After meandering a further 70 km (43 miles) upstream you will see the island of Koh Paen, 10 km (6 miles) long, in the middle of the Mekong. It is inhabited by Cham communities; as Sunni Muslims, their customs and dress are very different from those of their Cambodian neighbours. They once ruled an independent kingdom in Vietnam. By the 18th century they had been defeated by the Vietnamese, and many fled into this area of Cambodia.

Kampong Cham

You soon reach the easy-going town of Kampong Cham, in the midst of a region of rubber plantations on the west bank of the river. It is the largest town in the region, on the main road to Siem Reap. The Kizuna Bridge is a mark of the town's importance: it opened in 2001 and was the first across the Mekong to be built in Cambodia. The town is well worth strolling around for its small group of colonial era buildings.

Excursions include visits to rural Khmer villages such as **Prek Bang Kong**, **Angkor Ban** or the **Cheung Kok Ecotourism Village**, where you can see the villagers processing palm sugar and weaving *krama* scarves. Inland, about 7 km (4 miles) northwest of Kampong Cham, the well-preserved **Wat Nokor** (10th–16h centuries) has superbly carved reliefs. It is on the way to **Phnom Pros** and **Phnom Srei** (Man and Woman hills), which have given rise to many myths and legends. The trees are full of chattering monkeys, and there is a statue of the sacred bull Nandi.

Back on the river, about 20 km (12 miles) north of Kampong Cham, the ruins of the 8th-century **Phnom Han Chey** affords fine views over the Mekong. It is popular with Cambodian tourists and is surrounded by modern shrines and statues.

Kratie

After two great right-angle bends that change the course of the river, you reach the neat little town of Kratie, pronounced "Krat-chay". With some attractive French-era architecture, it's a highly appealing spot. A rapidly dwindling colony of Irrawaddy dolphins can be seen 12 km (7 miles) upriver at **Kampie**. These snub-nosed, rare dolphins grow up to almost 3 m in length and are distinguished by their small dorsal fins and bulbous foreheads.

Just north of Kratie, look out for the hilltop pagoda, **Phnom Sambok**. Climb the flight of steps here for a magnificent view of the Mekong and surrounding jungle.

You also get the opportunity to see them if you take a **Mekong Discovery Trail**, which can be tackled on motorbike or mountain bike and journeys through some of the poorest but friendliest areas of Cambodia, in all 180 km (112 miles) up to Stung (or Stœng) Treng near the border with Laos. A shorter bicycle circuit of 9 km (6 miles) is signposted on **Koh Trong**, an island that you can reach by ferry from Kratie's harbour. It has a beach, as well as a Vietnamese village in the south.

istockphoto.com/Highlanderimages

Mekong Wildlife. The river and its valley can claim to be one of the world's most remarkable stores of rare and unusual species of wildlife. Probably the best known of these are the Irrawaddy river dolphins, of which there are perhaps just a few hundred pairs still in existence. A small number can be seen just north of Kratie. In the Tonle Sap, the monster Giant Catfish weighs in at up to an impressive 350 kg, while the Mekong's freshwater stingrays can grow to a staggering 600 kg. In addition to these, naturalists have discovered more than a thousand new species of animals and plants in the Greater Mekong valley since the beginning of the 21st century. Among them are curious stripy rabbits, luminescent pink millipedes that make their own cyanide to keep predators at bay, and a rodent thought to have been extinct for 11 million years. Travellers on the river are always likely to see something rare and interesting, whatever form it might take.

A temple on stilts caters to the spiritual needs of the floating-village dwellers.

Tonle Sap Waterway

Other cruises from Phnom Penh take you to Siem Reap, gateway to the temples of Angkor. The modern town sits astride the Siem Reap River at the head of the vast Tonle Sap, a remarkable combined lake and river system whose flow changes direction twice a year, the lake shrinking and expanding with the seasons. Along the way, stops include the hilltop town of Udong, capital of Cambodia for almost 250 years. Charming floating villages and ancient temples dot the banks amid emerald-green ricefields.

Udong

About 35 km (22 miles) to the north of Phnom Penh, and 15 km (9 miles) inland from the west bank of the Tonle Sap River, Udong became the capital of Cambodia in 1618 after one of Phnom Penh's many periods of abandonment, and remained the royal stronghold until King Norodom re-established the capital at Phnom Penh in 1865. Its two ridges were once covered in temples, palaces and other important structures, though most have been destroyed or severely damaged, due in part to the fighting between government troops and the Khmer Rouge in the 1970s. Today Udong has become popular with weekend picnickers from the city, who appreciate the superb views of the countryside.

The smaller of the hills is topped by the bullet-riddled **Ta San Mosque** and the remnants of a large reclining Buddha, while the larger hill contains most of the points of interest. Its name—Phnom Preah Reach Troap—means "Hill of the Royal Fortune", as this is where the Khmer royal treasure was buried for safekeeping during the wars with the Siamese in the 16th century. The most striking building on the site is the restored **Preah Atharas**, a *vihara* dating from the reign of King Sisowath in the early 20th century that was blown up by the Khmer Rouge in 1977.

Preah Ko, 120 m north of here, contains a statue of Preah Ko itself, the sacred bull ridden by Shiva. Further on, **Neak Ta Dambang Dek** has a Buddha seated on a naga, here acting as his guardian.

Towards the end of the ridge stands a trio of older temples. **Chet Dey Mak Prohm** is distinctive for the four faces of Buddha on the cardinal points of its tower, recalling earlier Angkorian architecture. This stupa is also the burial place of King Monivong (reigned 1927–41). Next to it is **Tray Troeng**, built in 1891 to house the ashes of King Ang Duong. The oldest stupa in Udong, **Damrei Sam Poan**, dates from the 17th century and was the resting place of King Soriyopor.

It's worth entering the modern temple close by. This not only has the tallest spire on the hill but also boasts magnificent views all the way to the Tonle Sap River.

Kampong Tralach

The river snakes through the rice fields for 15 km (9 miles) towards this small town, heralded by **Wat Kampong Tralach Leu** just beyond the outskirts, a beautiful century-old temple with fine interior murals. It was in this area that King Ang Chan I established his capital, Lovek, in the 16th century, though its moment of glory was short-lived, as an invading Siamese army conquered it within a few decades. These days, Kampong Tralach provides a classic image of a rural Cambodian river town, where life moves at an enjoyably slow pace.

Kampong Chhnang

Another 60 km (37) miles to the north, the small port area of Kampong Chhnang might not at first seem very appealing, but head into the centre and you will be rewarded with a leafy town of French colonial architecture and a thriving local culture. The town lives mainly from fish farming but is named after the *chhnang*, the gold-tinted terracotta pots for which it is renowned throughout the country and which are often spotted being hauled on oxcarts and boats to distant locations. The handmade pots can be seen being produced by craftsmen in their houses at **Ondong Rossey**, a village 7 km (4 miles) northwest, reached by a pleasant ride through rice paddies.

You can get to the nearby floating villages of **Phumi Kandal** and **Chong Kos** by wooden boat from the Tourism Port. Like the workers in the rice paddies here, the fishermen are mainly ethnic Vietnamese and recognizable by their distinctive pointed hats.

Tonle Sap Lake

A short distance from Kampong Chhnang, the narrow funnel of the river enters the lake at its southeast corner. With a length of 160 km (100 miles), the lake can seem as vast as an ocean during the crossing.

This is no ordinary lake. In the dry season it's a swampy area of some 2,700 sq km (1,042 sq miles), but when the rains hit Cambodia in June, the Tonle Sap River, which runs out from its southern end, reverses its flow. The lake quickly swells to an enormous 12,000 sq km (4,633 sq miles), and rises by up to nine times its usual depth of 1 m, becoming the largest body of fresh water in Southeast Asia. The cause of this phenomenon is the Mekong River, filling up with snow melt and runoff from the monsoon rains. It backs up into the Tonle Sap at the confluence and forces the waters of the river up into the lake. The forested plain becomes flooded: if you are sailing on it during high water, the plants you see as you look down are in fact the tops of submerged trees. The practicality of the floating villages of stilt houses becomes all too apparent, as they are able simply to move with the incredible inrush of water. For the local people it acts as a floodplain, reservoir, rice-paddy irrigator, transport system and fishery, providing all the necessities of life as it has done since the great days of Angkor. It provides more than 75 per cent of the country's annual inland fish catch. When the flow reverses at the end of the rainy season, the fish are carried downriver. The system supports more than 100 varieties of waterbirds, over 200 species of fish, as well as crocodiles, turtles, otter, and other wildlife in the mangrove forest.

On the eastern shore, **Kampong Khleang** is the largest community on the lake with a population of 30,000 living in a veritable forest of stilt houses. Further north, **Kampong Phluk** is a cluster of three Khmer villages shared between 10,000 inhabitants. The closest floating village to Siem Reap, and the one that gets most visitors, is **Chong Khneas**; boat tours come here from the city every day and include stops at a fish and bird exhibition and a gecko centre.

At the northwest tip of the lake, the **Prek Toal Bird Sanctuary** is home to rare and endangered species including spot-billed pelicans, black-headed ibis and grey-headed fish eagles. If you visit during the dry season, the reduced volume of water means that a greater number of birds can be seen in a smaller area.

Siem Reap

The boats from Phnom Penh anchor below **Phnom Krom**, on the north shore of the Tonle Sap, though in the dry season they have to weigh further out. The town lies 15 km (9 miles) north of the lake on the Siem Reap River. Laid out in grid-pattern form, Siem Reap (pronounced See-am Ree-up) is the fastest-growing town in Cambodia, with new 5-star hotels and spas, an abundance of air-conditioned restaurants and bars, and clean, modern streets.

It's hard to believe that, until relatively recently, this was a sleepy backwater, living off the abundant fishing and rice production from the flood plains of the Tonle Sap lake as it had done for centuries. The reason for the transformation is that this is the gateway town for the world-renowned Angkor archaeological

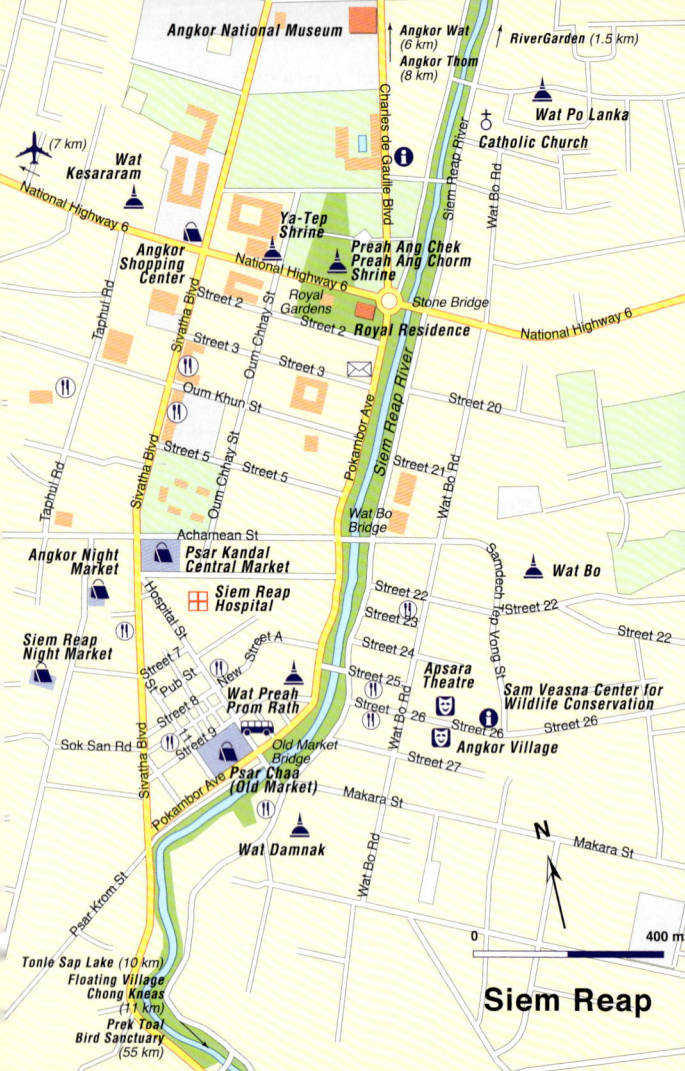

site and its multitude of international visitors. However, Siem Reap and its environs are worth investigating beyond the nightspots where visitors chill out after a hot day wandering around Angkor's magnificent temples.

Probably the best place to start any encounter with the life of the town is at one of its markets. The biggest and liveliest, at the southern end of Siem Reap, next to the river, is **Psar Chas** (Old Market), which offers Cambodian shopping at its most full-blooded. On sale are gold and silver jewellery, gems, silk items, rattan baskets and mats, and fresh exotic food, with bustling cafés and bars.

From here, head north along the pleasant riverside walk towards the centre of town. After around 300 m, turn right and cross the river onto Achamean Street. Continue along here to **Wat Bo**, the oldest temple in Siem Reap. It was founded in the 18th century, though the superb frescoes depicting scenes from the Buddha's life date from a century later. Look out for the unusual inclusion of a group of French soldiers at a dance performance in one of them.

Back on the west side of the river, carry on northwards past the main post office to the **Royal Gardens**. This delightful oasis is a great place to cool off and escape the noise and traffic of the town.

Further up from the gardens on Avenue Charles de Gaulle is the **Angkor National Museum**, which covers all periods of the Angkor site. Using sculptures and other artefacts once hidden away at the Angkor Conservatory, it gives a useful introduction to the history and meaning of the extraordinary sights to be encountered just a few kilometres away. Exhibits are labelled in English, French, Thai and Khmer.

Outside Siem Reap

Call in at the **Tonle Sap Exhibition** on the road to Angkor Wat just past the Jayavarman VII hospital. Sponsored by an organization assisting children, it has informative displays including maps and photos, models of traditional houses, boats and fishing implements. A working model of the lake helps you understand its unique environment.

This region was one of the last strongholds of the Khmer Rouge and as such still suffers from the effects of landmines laid by their army. On the far side of Angkor, towards the Banteay Srei temple, the **Landmine Museum** maintains a serious, if slightly eccentric, approach to the issue, with displays of mines, bombs and artillery, the chance to search out (deactivated) mines in the garden, and a film on how the problem affects the lives of local people.

The five mighty towers of Angkor Wat have come to symbolize the Cambodian people's cultural pride and identity.

The Angkor Sites

Located north of the Tonle Sap lake, the Unesco listed Angkor temples are the vestiges of religious constructions in stone from a dozen different Khmer capitals and their satellite cities. Built and rebuilt between the 9th and 16th centuries, the ensemble comprises a thousand monuments spread over as many square kilometres.

Some are reduced to rubble, impossible to identify. The most spectacular, such as Angkor Wat and the Bayon, were built between the 10th and 13th centuries and are mainly concentrated in an area of 50 sq km (19 sq miles) north of Siem Reap. This cluster is Angkor proper, though its true name is Yashodharapura, as Angkor merely means "city", and Wat "temple".

Most of the visitors to Angkor head for Siem Reap for lunch, though restaurants and takeaways are lined up opposite the entrance to Angkor Wat, and there are noodle stalls near the main temples.

Angkor Wat

Protected by a massive moat and outer walls, and reached by a long causeway, the temple-mountain of Angkor Wat is undoubtedly the masterpiece of Khmer architecture. Unlike most of the buildings at Angkor, it seems to have been in continual use by Buddhist monks since the area was largely abandoned in the 15th century. However, when the temple was built in the first half of the 12th century under King Suryavarman II, it was dedicated to the Hindu god Vishnu. It's the only temple to face west. This is probably because Vishnu was identified with the west, but also suggests that it was intended to be used as the king's mausoleum.

Make sure you leave enough time to pore over the magnificent bas-reliefs that stretch for 800 m around the wall of the temple. Packed with movement and a thrilling sense of drama, they depict scenes from the Hindu epics, the *Mahabarata* and the *Ramayana*, as well as events from the reign of Suryavarman II. Look out, too, for the evocative Heavens and Hells gallery, and the splendid Churning of the Ocean of Milk, where gods and devils play tug-of-war using a serpent to see who will win immortality. Hundreds of Apsara dancers grace the walls with their eternal beauty.

Phnom Bakheng

Take the trouble to climb (though you can ride up on an elephant) Phnom Bakheng, just north of Angkor Wat. The 9th-century five-tiered temple on the mountain was founded during the reign of Yasovarman I and was the first of its kind to be built in Angkor. Huge crowds come here at sunset, but the best time to go is early morning, when you can have the place to yourself.

Angkor Thom

Following the capture of Angkor in a surprise attack by the Chams in 1177, Jayavarman VII founded a new and final city not far from Angkor Wat. The colossal Angkor Thom (literally, Great City) forms a defensive rectangular flanked by a moat; each laterite wall is 3 km (1.8 miles) long and 8 m high. The perimeter is interspersed with five imposing gates. The city is usually entered through the south gate, towered over by the smiling face of Avalokitésvara, avatar of ultimate compassion.

Bayon

In the centre of Angkor Thom rises the breathtaking temple-mountain of the Bayon, where the distinction between architecture and sculpture disappears. Despite its ruined condition and the undoubted architectural problems caused when a third level was superimposed on the second,

---

A civilization built on water. The monuments of Angkor were closely tied to a complex system of irrigation that made use of immense artificial reservoirs known as barays, and earned for the Khmer capital the name of "hydraulic city". In fact, building a successful city-state in Asia, where the monsoon rains are so unevenly distributed, necessarily involved stocking water to be shared out evenly over the course of the seasons, and thus ensuring a good, regular harvest. This hydraulic network was developed in a particularly genial location in the fertile plain between the Phnom Kulen hills to the north and the fish-breeding Tonle Sap lake to the south. The linchpin of the empire, the reservoir system became a genuine machine for intensive cereal production, assuring two or three crops per year—enough to supply the 1 million people who lived in the capital as workers, forced labourers and soldiers. But the over-exploitation of the fragile land, combined with deforestation, impoverished the earth, clogged up and dried out the hydraulic network. By the 14th century, the kings of Angkor were finding it hard to nourish their people, and in the face of intensifying attacks by the Thais, abandoned their monumental city. Declining economically, deprived of its political functions, deserted little by little by its "urban" population, Angkor largely returned to the forest, not to be cleared of the overgrowth of trees and foliage until archaeologists and tourists began arriving in the late 19th century.

cramping the courtyards and galleries, it retains an extraordinarily enigmatic and exotic power. The level of artistic creativity in evidence here is awesome, with richly carved bas-reliefs and a forest of 54 towers showing the heads of Buddha that significantly resemble Jayavarman VII himself.

Baphuon

Its restoration partly completed, the nearby Baphuon belongs to an earlier city on this site. Built in the 11th century by King Udayadityavarman II, it's another temple-mountain and represents the mythical Mount Meru.

Royal Palace

To the north, in front of a vast square delineated by a row of twelve laterite towers, the royal palace has been reduced over time to its foundations. On the façade is the **Terrace of the Elephants**, with a marvellous bas-relief procession of tuskers. Just along from here, the statue of the Leper King on the terrace is a copy—the original is displayed in the National Museum in Phnom Penh. Archaeologists have still not determined whether it represents one of the Angkorian kings or the god of death. The raised platform itself was probably used for ceremonial cremations. Hidden behind it, a wall reached by a narrow passage reveals hundreds of deities.

Around Angkor

Surrounding Angkor Wat and Angkor Thom are numerous ancient temples in varying states of repair. The best can be seen on two main circuits, the Great Circuit of 25 km (15.5 miles) and the Small Circuit of 15 km (9 miles), easily reached by tuk-tuk on relatively good roads.

Preah Khan

Just north of the city walls of Angkor Thom, the university-monastery of Preah Khan was consecrated in 1191 by Jayavarman VII in honour of his father. It's a vast complex, still partially covered by vegetation, with a maze of courtyards and corridors. In the northeastern part of the monastery, look out for a remarkable two-storey structure which, with its classical columns and carvings, might easily have been transported here from Ancient Rome.

Western Mebon

Built around 953 in honour of god Shiva, this 11th century mountain-temple located 4 km (2.4 miles) west of Angkor Tom is notable for the lions and elephants sculptures guarding its superimposed terraces.

Ta Prohm

Jayavarman VII was clearly a dutiful son, for the Ta Prohm

At Ta Prohm, the trees are slowly asserting their rights over the crumbling monuments.

monastery, just west of Banteay Kdei, this time commemorates his mother. Dating from 1186, it housed a monastery and a Buddhist university. Archaeologists made a deliberate decision to leave Ta Prohm as they found it, and so it offers a rare chance to see how Angkor looked when the first Europeans arrived in the 19th century. It's a breathtaking sight. With trees emerging out of temple buildings, and thick roots covering ruined passageways and courtyards, the jungle here has become part of the architecture.

Banteay Kdei

The late-12th-century Banteay Kdei is a Buddhist temple with a real lost-city atmosphere. As you enter, a great sight of endlessly receding doorways with carvings of Apsaras draws you inside. Leave at the far end and you'll come to a raised stone platform with a superb view over the Srah Srang pond, which was possibly used as a pool for ritualized bathing.

Prasat Kravan

The striking red-brick temples of Prasat Kravan are among the oldest in Angkor and date from 921. They were built as Hindu temples, and inside them are fine bas-reliefs of Vishnu and his consort, Lakshmi.

Roluos Group

The city of Hariharalaya, one of the first great symbols of Khmer culture, was built in the 9th century under Indravarman I.

Located some 15 km (9 miles) east of Siem Reap, it stretched to the south of the Baray of Lolei, or Indratataka, nearly 4 km (2.5 miles) long by 700 m (half a mile) wide. The surviving structures are referred to today as the Roluos group.

The heart of the city was the ancestral temple of **Preah Ko** (880), which housed the statues of the ancient king-protectors of the empire, and the magnificent temple-mountain of the **Bakong**. Built in 881 and surrounded by large moats, this was dedicated to the Hindu god, Shiva, and with its high central tower—a design that would reach its peak in Angkor Wat—is a symbolic representation of Mount Meru.

Constructed on an island in the middle of the baray—which has now disappeared—the red-sandstone towers of **Lolei temple** (889) were also intended for Hindu worship. They were consecrated to the memory of the founder of the city by his son, Yasovarman I. Nowadays a modern temple and a community of monks inhabit it anew.

Banteay Srei

This small temple was built some 20 km (12 miles) upstream from Angkor during the 10th century. It was off-limits to visitors for many years because Khmer Rouge bandits were operating in the region, but it is now a safe and very popular side trip. It's distinguished by the colour—a glorious pink sandstone. An entrance path leads to the three main towers enclosed on a charming islet surrounded by moats. The main sanctuary is guarded by mythological monkey-headed figures, and the carvings are beautifully detailed and decorated.

Kbal Spien

The famous River of a Thousand Lingas, 10 km (6 miles) further on, is a tranquil spot in which to view an intriguing array of 11th-century rock carvings—phalli, symbols of fertility, and later representations of Shiva and Vishnou.

Phnom Kulen

This is Cambodia's most sacred mountain, where in 802, Jayavarman II proclaimed himself the first god-king of Angkor. It's a tough, two-hour haul to the top, where you'll find a pagoda near a spring which is the source of the Tonle Sap lake. A thousand stone phalluses are sculpted in the riverbed, as well as an elaborate carving of Vishnu (Jayavarman had parts of the river diverted to reveal the sandstone floor).

How to visit Angkor? You'll need to arrange transport in order to get around the temples—motorcycle taxi *(motodup)* or trailer *(remorque-moto* or *tuk-tuk)*, car taxi, or bicycle (electric or pedal-powered). The entire area is well organized and served by good roads. You can enter by buying an Angkor Pass for 1, 3 or 7 days. The 3- and 7-day passes are valid for 1 week and 1 month respectively. They can be bought at the entrance.

The site is open from sunrise to sunset. There's a staggering number of buildings worth seeing, and it would take a week to visit most of them. Those described in this chapter comprise all the main temples in and around Angkor, and can be comfortably covered within 3 days.

Rice is Cambodia's major crop, with at least two harvests per year, one in monsoon season, one in dry season.

West Cambodia

Travelling around the country has become much easier in recent years, with plenty of comfortable express buses. You can also reach places such as Battambang by boat, or go further afield by internal flights. The delightful seaside resort of Sihanoukville can be reached from Phnom Penh on the American-built Highway 4 in just a few hours by air-conditioned coach.

Sihanoukville

The town grew up around the port of Kampong Som on the Gulf of Thailand, itself established in 1955 following Cambodian independence.

Take a boat to the tranquil little islands of **Koh Tang** and **Koh Rong**. Their waters are popular with divers. Koh Tang has an unusual claim to fame as the location of the last battle of the Vietnam War in 1975, when the US fought with Khmer Rouge troops here.

Ream National Park, 20 km (12 miles) from Sihanoukville, has been a protected area since 1993. Dolphins swim along its island-studded coastline and there's some beautiful coral in the sea.

Kep

The seaside resort east of Sihanoukville was founded in 1908 as a retreat for the French elite. Evacuated by the Khmer Rouge, its luxurious Modernist villas have long stood as blackened shells, abandoned to squatters. The town is now undergoing a revival, drawing Khmer families to the beaches and more affluent visitors to its boutique hotels.

Battambang

Cambodia's second city is an attractive town with some of the country's finest colonial architecture. Rice paddies dominate the landscape all the way to the Thai border. A walk along the River Sangker allows you to see many of the French shop houses once used by colonial traders. This area comes alive at night and is packed with food and drink stalls.

Near the river, **Battambang Museum** displays a collection of items from the region's temples.

The former **Governor's House** to the south is arguably the most splendid colonial building in Cambodia.

Phnom Sampeau to the southwest is a spectacular outcrop, with 600 steps to the temple on the top, as well as a couple of large field guns—this was an outpost of the Phnom Penh government's battle against Khmer Rouge rebels until late 1996.

On a hilltop 20 km (12 miles) south of town is the 10th-century **Wat Banan** temple. With five laterite and sandstone towers, it conjures up something of the flavour of Angkor Wat.

Lengths of silk embroidered in gold thread, with elephants and geometrical designs.

SHOPPING

A shopping trip to one of the busy markets in Phnom Penh or Siem Reap is undoubtedly one of the most entertaining experiences Cambodia has to offer. Here, the everyday process of buying and selling becomes a full-blooded participation sport.

Psar Thmei, the vast Central Market in Phnom Penh, is packed with stalls selling cut gems and gold and silver items (beware of counterfeit jewellery). There are also solid-colour lengths, sometimes with moiré effect. In the southern part of the city, the Russian Market is a good place for discounted or made-to-measure clothes and for silk and jewellery, but beware of counterfeit products. Foulards are sold in bundles and all sorts of traditional Cambodian and Vietnamese souvenirs can also be found. The Old Market in Siem Reap has as many Angkor-influenced sculptures as you could want.

Fine copies of Angkorian bronzes are sometimes found on sale in the National Museum shop in Phnom Penh, cast according to traditional methods by old masters. You might also consider buying souvenir and handicraft items made by disabled victims of Cambodia's landmines. These can be found in shops set up by NGOs in the main cities.

Handwoven silk is first-rate. Silk is sold by the length—sufficient for a Khmer man's *sarong* or woman's *sampot* (skirt). If you take a close look at any of the female statues in the museums, you'll see they are all wearing *sampots*. The plaid-like fabrics are reserved for men. Also look for other items made from silk, such as bags and purses. Very popular is also the traditional scarf known as a *krama*. Made from silk or cotton, it's used by locals to keep the sun off their heads and dust out of their eyes.

Cambodian artisans were famous throughout the region for their skills. They were almost entirely wiped out under the Khmer Rouge, but some survived to keep the tradition going, and today there is a considerable amount of finely worked jewellery and silverware to be found. Be careful if you want to buy gold: it's often just plated.

DINING OUT

Khmer cuisine has a long tradition of excellence dating back to the time when it was considered one of the fine arts of the royal court. At its best, it can hold its own with the more famous neighbouring cuisines of Thailand and Vietnam. Using aromatic herbs such as lemongrass, tamarind, coriander and mint, seasoned with a complex multitude of spices, it provides a delicious way of discovering an essential aspect of Cambodian culture.

You can sample Khmer cooking in a variety of different establishments, ranging from food stalls in the market to elegant restaurants in downtown Phnom Penh. You'll also find any amount of good, inexpensive cooking from around the region, in particular Chinese and Thai food. What's more, old ties with the former colonial ruler haven't completely dissolved, and along with baguettes and croissants, the main towns boast some first-rate French restaurants.

Main Courses

Freshwater fish features heavily in Khmer cuisine, courtesy of the vast amount produced in the great Tonle Sap lake and the Mekong River. Seafood comes from the coast on the Gulf of Thailand. The staple is rice, *bai*. One of Cambodia's great specialities is *trei ang*, grilled fish which is usually dipped in *teuk trei*, a fish sauce used to salt food. Other mouthwatering dishes include *trei chamhoy*, steamed whole fish, *trei neung phkea*, served with shrimps, and *trei chean neung spei*, fried with vegetables.

Be sure to try *amok*, a delicious curry of poached catfish in a rich coconut sauce considered to be the national dish. It is usually served in banana leaves. You may also be curious to taste the more rustic dried (*ngeat*) or smoked (*chha'ae*) fish, fermented fish dishes (*prahok*, *nam*)—or even fried spiders or rolled snake. The prawns are recommended, as is *khao poun*, rice noodles with pork in a coconut sauce.

As for salads, *phlea sach ko* is composed of vegetables mixed with beef marinated in lemon juice; *ngom moan* is a chicken salad, *ngom trei* is the fish version.

Most dishes are accompanied by *samla*, a substantial soup. *Samla mchou banle* is a piquant fish-based soup with a slightly sour flavour, while spicy *samla mchou bangkang* has prawns as the main ingredient. The tasty *samla kroueung* resembles a beef stew. Look out also for *samla chapek*, with pork and ginger, and *samla kti*, a pork, chicken or fish soup with coconut milk and pineapple.

Desserts and Drinks

Desserts (*bangaem*) are mainly reserved for festival days or religious offerings. However, if you like to finish off your meals on a sweet note, you'll find all sorts of pastries (*noum*) as well as rice or fruit cakes, taro puddings, flambé bananas and little eggy cakes that are sold at street stalls.

Tea and coffee are always available—the coffee is often iced and served with sweetened condensed milk. Fresh fruit drinks (*tikaloks*) are made at street stalls; if you prefer them unsweetened say so, or they'll have plenty of sugar added. Coconut juice is cool and will be opened before your eyes.

Many restaurants in Phnom Penh and Siem Reap have extensive wine lists. Cambodian beer such as Angkor is excellent.

THE HARD FACTS

Airports
Phnom Penh International Airport is situated 8 km (5 miles) west of the city; Siem Reap airport is 7 km (4 miles) outside town and serves tourists wanting to visit Angkor.

The terminals have fairly limited tourist information services, cafés, currency exchange and duty-free facilities. If you do not already have special arrangements made for the journey into town (some hotels offer a free pick-up service, for example), you'll find plenty of taxi drivers outside the terminal clamouring for your custom. If you don't want to haggle over price, you can buy a pre-paid voucher before leaving the building.

Climate
Cambodia has a tropical climate, with a southwest monsoon bringing heavy afternoon rains between mid-May and beginning of October and a dry season from November to April. The coolest month of the year is January when the daily average temperature is 28°C (82.4°F); the hottest is April, with temperatures reaching 40°C (104°F). From July to September, during the wettest months of the monsoon, roads can become impassable, and travel around the country might be difficult.

Communications
The postal service in Cambodia is relatively efficient. If you want to mail a parcel, send it registered. Along with selling stamps and phonecards, main post offices offer telephone, fax, e-mail and poste restante facilities. The main post office in Phnom Penh is on Street 13 and corner of Street 102; at Siem Reap it's on the west side of the river south of the Grand Hotel d'Angkor.

International telephone calls are cheaper if made at the post office rather than from your hotel, and there's a significant reduction for calls made at the weekend. Camintel and Mobitel phonecards can be bought from shops and hotels as well as the post office, and used in any of the public phone booths in the cities.

To call overseas, dial 001 or 007 + country code + area code (minus the initial 0) + local number. The country code for Cambodia if you are dialling from abroad is 855; the city code for Phnom Penh is 023, Siem Reap 063, Sihanoukville 034.

Faxes can be sent and received at hotels, but are also expensive.

The internet is very popular in Cambodia, and it's the cheapest way of regularly keeping in touch with people at home. There are plenty of Internet cafés, and more and more hotels and post offices also offer free Wi-Fi facilities.

Driving
Self-driving is considered to be dangerous, especially in the cities, and few rental companies hand out vehicles without a chauffeur. In any case, being driven around by a local professional is the wisest option: apart from the newest highways, the condition of many roads still leaves a lot to be desired, and there seem to be no traffic rules at all.

A motorbike provides independence and flexibility, but tourists are no longer allowed to hire them in Siem Reap, where there have been too many accidents. In other places, weigh up very carefully the dangers of travelling on unfamiliar Cambodian roads and through crowded city streets.

Emergencies
Emergency phone numbers:
police: 117
fire: 118
ambulance: 119
For the Tourism Police, where English is certain to be spoken dial 023 724 793 or 012 942 484. However, most problems can be handled at your hotel desk. The European Dental Clinic is on 023 211 363 or 012 893 174 (emergency number 012 986 024). Serious medical problems will probably entail evacuation to Bangkok—the International SOS Medical Clinic can arrange these on 023 216 911 or 012 816 911.

Etiquette
It is considered impolite to point one's finger at people or at statues of Buddha, and also to show the soles of one's feet or shoes. Do not pat children on the head, or even touch adults on the head. When handing or receiving anything, always use your right hand or both hands (which is considered more polite). Have a few coloured pencils ready in your pockets for children, instead of giving them money or sweets. Cover your shoulders and knees when visiting a royal or religious site.

Formalities
You will need a passport, valid for at least six months after your date of arrival, and a visa, which can be obtained online: evisa.mfaic.gov.kh. One-month tourist visas are also issued on arrival. Beware of fake visa sites, and note that not all the customs and entry points accept e-visas, so check the official website before leaving. Remember to

Be sure to interpret the signs properly—this one is for the vet.

bring a passport-size photo of yourself. The officials at Phnom Penh Airport have a camera at the ready if you have forgotten to bring one, but will charge you for the service.

Health

You need a travel insurance that includes medical cover and have all necessary immunizations—contact your doctor or travel centre to find out what's required. Malaria occurs across the whole country apart from Phnom Penh and the Tonle Sap lake region. An antimalarial treatment prior to departure is advisable, but preventing the insects getting to you is best, though, so it's a good idea to carry mosquito repellent cream, and keep arms and legs covered in the evenings.

It's wise to avoid too much exposure to the sun. Wear a hat, use a good sun-screen and keep in the shade as much as possible, especially in the middle of the day. Drink plenty of mineral water to avoid dehydration—but never tap water. Avoid salad and fruit that's been washed in unpurified water, ice cubes and fruit juice diluted with tap water—and brush your teeth in mineral water.

If you require specialized prescription medicines, remember to take enough with you to last for the duration of your stay.

Holidays and festivals

Many of Cambodia's public holidays and festivals follow the lunar calendar, moving from year to year. During all of the following holidays, you'll find banks and offices shut. At Cambodian New Year virtually the entire country is on the move, with most of the population seeming to head for the temples at Angkor.

Jan 1	New Year's Day
Jan 7	Victory Day
March 8	Women's Day
May 1	Labour Day
May 15	King Sihamoni's Birthday
May 20	Day of Remembrance
June 18	Former Queen's Birthday
Sept 24	Constitution Day
Oct 29	Coronation Day
Oct 31	Former King Sihanouk's Birthday
Nov 9	Independence Day
Dec 10	Human Rights' Day

Moveable festivals:
February: *Bon Meak Bochea* (Commemoration of Buddha's funeral)
Mid-April: *Bon Chaul Chnam* (Cambodian New Year)
April/May: *Visaka Bochea* (Buddha's Birthday)
April/May: *Bon Chrott Preah Nongkoal* (Royal Ploughing Day Ceremony)
Sept/Oct: *Pchum Ben* (Spirits Commemoration Festival)
November: *Bon Om Touk* Water and Moon Festival marking the reverse flow of the Tonle Sap at the start of the dry season.

Language

The majority of Cambodians speak Khmer, a non-tonal language which theoretically makes it easier for Westerners to speak. English is widely understood, especially by younger people, and French is still often spoken in touristic areas.

Media

There are plenty of locally published English-language papers and magazines to choose from. The *Cambodia Daily* covers both national and international news and has a useful What's On section on Friday. The daily *Phnom Penh Post* provides a well-written overview of Cambodian news and local interest stories. International newspapers or magazines such as *Bangkok Post* and the *International New York Times* can be found in the cities.

Most medium- and top-range hotels have satellite TV, showing BBC, CNN, French and Japanese channels. Short-wave radio enthusiasts can listen to BBC World Service, Voice of America and Radio Australia. The BBC World Service is also broadcast locally on 100.0 FM radio.

Money matters

The unit of currency in Cambodia is the *riel*; the most frequently used banknotes are 1000, 2000, 5000, 10,000, 20,000, 50,000 and 100,000 riel. You're not likely to see any coins. The US dollar is used as a day-to-day part of the Cambodian monetary system. In the west of the country, Thai *baht* are also generally accepted.

Given that this is almost completely a cash economy with credit cards taken at only the most expensive hotels and restaurants (though even this is changing, and banks such as Mekong Bank have launched their own Visa card), it makes sense to bring enough money in low denomination US dollar bills (in good condition) to cover such things as meals, travel and shopping for the duration of your holiday. That being said, here are now ATMs in most towns where you can withdraw dollars.

If you do bring other currencies, make sure you don't change too much into riels: it is not a convertible currency and banks and exchange bureaux won't buy back your unspent riels when you leave the country.

Opening hours

Banks are generally open from Monday to Friday from 8 a.m. to 3 p.m. or 4 p.m., Saturday to 11.30 or noon.

The main post offices in Phnom Penh and Siem Reap are open every day from 7 a.m. to 6 p.m. and 5.30 p.m. respectively.

There are no set hours for shops, though they tend to open daily, start early and close any time from early evening through till late.

Government offices: from 7.30 or 8 a.m. to 11.30 a.m. and from 2 p.m. to 5 or 5.30 p.m.

Museums keep less demanding times, opening daily from around 8 a.m. to 5 p.m.; some of them make a long break for lunch.

Temples open from 5 or 7 a.m. to 6 p.m.

Photography

Remember that the tropical light is at its best for a couple of hours after sunrise and just before sunset, and very harsh from mid-morning to mid-afternoon. When taking people's photographs, ask for their permission first.

Public Transport

Cambodia's public transport system is in the throes of development, but the road network has been vastly improved in recent years. Comfortable buses, often air-conditioned, travel the main highways—and not only the excellent Highway 4 from Phnom Penh to the beach resort at Sihanoukville and Highway 6 from Phnom Penh to Siem Reap. Several bus companies operate between Phnom Penh and Siem Reap, each leaving 3 to 4 times a day. Buses also go from the capital to Battambang, Sihanoukville, Kampot and even Bangkok and Saigon. Phnom Penh Sorya transport company also serves a few smaller cities. You can generally arrange for excursions at your hotel or guest house.

Since the roads have been improved, river transport has been reduced or even abandoned. You can still take an express boat up the Tonle Sap river and across the Tonle Sap lake to Phnom Krom, from where you can hire a taxi to Siem Reap. It's an enjoyable 4-hour ride, although when the water is low during the dry season and smaller speedboats have to be used, it can also be a rather hair-raising one as well.

The most practical and inexpensive way to get around town is by *moto* (or *motodup*) a motorcycle taxi. The two-seater motorcycle taxi is called *remorque-kang* but these are rapidly dwindling. In Phnom Penh, Siem Reap and Sihanoukville you'll see *remorque-motos* with small two-seater canopied trailers; they are also called *tuk-tuks* by foreigners. The normal *remorque-moto* is a large trailer hitched to a motorcycle and can transport large groups of people, but as they are not allowed into the cities. The *cyclo*, or cycle-rickshaw, the more traditional South-East Asian mode of transport, is becoming rarer. There are some taxi cars available, especially at the airports. If you prefer to use one of these at other times, ask your hotel desk.

Safety
Cambodia is now a country at peace, and visitors will generally find that Cambodians are friendly and helpful towards them. This doesn't mean that precautions shouldn't be taken. In Phnom Penh especially, make sure valuables are kept in the hotel safe. Carry cash in a money belt or sealable pocket, and be especially vigilant in crowded places where pickpockets operate. Be careful not to stray too far off the beaten track alone at night. And above all, if you're out in the countryside—including the area around the temples at Angkor—be aware that landmines laid by the Khmer Rouge rebels up to the mid-1990s are still a problem. Keep to designated paths, and never wander off into the jungle without a guide.

Time
Standard time in Cambodia is UTC/GMT+7, all year round.

Tipping
While tipping isn't customary in Cambodia, bear in mind that wages are extremely low and a tip for good service will generally be highly appreciated.

Toilets
You won't find many public toilets on your travels, so whenever you're in tourist-friendly places such as cafés, restaurants, hotels and museums, remember to take advantage of the facilities!

Tourist Information Offices
You might be able to elicit answers to basic questions about the country, but you're likely to come away knowing little more than when you went in. The tourist office at Phnom Penh Airport should be able to offer help about accommodation when you arrive.

Voltage
Electric current is generally 220V, 50 cycle A.C., and sockets are for plugs with two round pins. Power cuts can be frequent. Bring a torch just in case.

INDEX

Angkor 111–115
Angkor Ban 102
Angkor Thom 112–113
    Baphuon 113
    Bayon 112–113
    Royal Palace 113
Angkor Wat 111–112
Bakong 114
Banteay Kdei 114
Banteay Srei 115
Battambang 117
Chong Khneas 107
Chong Kos 106
Cheung Kok 102
Kampie 103
Kampong Cham 102
Kampong Chhnang 106
Kampong Khleang 107
Kampong Phluk 107
Kampong Tralach 106
Kbal Spien 115
Kep 117
Koh Chen 101
Koh Dach 101
Koh Paen 101
Koh Trong 103
Kratie 103
Lolei 115
Mekong 101–103
Mekong Discovery Trail 103
Mekong Wildlife 103
Ondong Rossey 106
Phnom Bakheng 111–112
Phnom Chisor 99
Phnom Kulen 115
Phnom Krom 107
Phnom Penh 93–98
    Central Market (Psar Thmei) 97
    Colonial Quarter 98
    Independence Monument 97
    Killing Fields of Choeung Ek 98
    National Museum 94–95
    Palace quarter 93–95
    Royal Palace 94
    Russian Market (Psar Toul Tom Poung) 98
    Silver Pagoda 94
    Sisowath Quay 95–97
    Toul Sleng Museum 98
    Wat Ounalom 97
    Wat Phnom 97
Phnom Pros 102
Phnom Sambok 103
Phnom Sampeau 117
Phnom Srei 102
Phumi Kandal 106
Prasat Kravan 114
Preah Khan 103
Preah Ko 114
Prek Bang Kong 102
Prek Toal Bird Sanctuary 107
Ream National Park 117
Roluos Group 114–115
Siem Reap 107–109
Sihanoukville 117
Ta Prohm monastery 113–114
Ta Prohm temple 99
Tonle Bati 99
Tonle Sap 105–109
Tonle Sap Lake 106–107
Udong 105–106
Wat Banan 117
Wat Nokor 102
Wat Hanchey 102
Western Mebon 113
Yeay Peau 99

Editor
Eleonora Di Campli

Corrections and Revisions
Claude Hervé-Bazin
Theresa Lachner

Design
Karin Palazzolo

Layout
Luc Malherbe
Matias Jolliet

Photo credits
p. 81: hemis.fr/Boisberranger
p. 82: istockphoto.com/kbubbs (prayer flags); /Mette (Lotus flowers); /Freeman (Ta Prohm); fotolia.com/Arraial (market sellers on the Mekong)

Maps
JPM Publications,
Mathieu Germay

Copyright © 2014
JPM Publications S.A.
12, avenue William-Fraisse,
1006 Lausanne, Suisse
information@jpmguides.com
http://www.jpmguides.com/

All rights reserved. No part of this book may be reproduced or transmitted in any form or by any means, electronic or mechanical, including photocopying, recording or by any information storage and retrieval system without permission in writing from the publisher.

Every care has been taken to verify the information in the guide, but the publisher cannot accept responsibility for any errors that may have occurred. If you spot an inaccuracy or a serious omission, please let us know.

Printed in Switzerland
15162.00.15377
Edition 2014

LAOS

Dan Colwell

JPMGUIDES

a well-kept secret

CONTENTS

131	This Way Laos
135	Flashback
141	On The Scene
141	Vientiane
149	Luang Prabang
155	The South
159	Shopping
160	Dining Out
162	The Hard Facts
168	Index

Fold-out map
Laos
Luang Prabang
Vientiane

splendid architecture

welcoming smiles

Buddhist and animist faith

THIS WAY LAOS

This was once Lan Xang, the Kingdom of a Million Elephants. Enclosed by mountains, hemmed in by China, Vietnam, Cambodia, Thailand and Myanmar, it long remained a well-kept secret. The kingdom declined in the 19th century and was almost swallowed up by the Siamese empire, until the French took over the region and re-established the old borders along the Mekong River.

In more recent times, the Vietnam War and a socialist revolution have conspired to wrench Laos out of the past.

An unshakeable otherworldliness remains, despite the transformation that has occurred since Laos began opening up to the outside world at the end of the 1980s. Many despise the plague of modernism, and throw up their hands in horror at the soulless, contemporary buildings that have sprouted on the city skylines. But the concept of modernity has always been relative here. Wander around the quiet streets of Luang Prabang, the ancient royal capital, in the early morning and you'll find that the pervading peace is broken only by the sound of gongs coming from ancient temples, or the soft sound of bare feet on stone, as saffron-robed Buddhist monks pad along in single file collecting alms from citizens seated cross-legged on the ground. Visit the country's most modern metropolis, Vientiane, and it will seem a sleepy little spot after the rumbustious mayhem of Phnom Penh or the economic dynamism of Bangkok. Though low-key by South-East Asian standards, it serves as a perfect introduction to the easygoing Laotian way of life.

Wherever you find yourself in this land of beauty and tradition, the cultural ambience of Lan Xang never seems far away.

The Land

A long, thin sliver wedged into the middle of Indochina, Laos—officially the Lao People's Democratic Republic (Lao PDR)—is topographically complex and entirely landlocked. It's slightly larger than Great Britain, which

Wall painting in Vientiane, a reminder of the days when Laos was the Kingdom of a Million Elephants.

makes it extremely spacious in relation to its 6.8 million population, with a ratio of only 27 people per sq km. Given that 90 per cent of the land is mountainous, it's no surprise to find that the vast majority live along the banks of the Mekong.

The River

One of Asia's greatest rivers, the Mekong rises in Qinghai Province, China, and flows southwards through Tibet and into Laos, forming its border with Myanmar and Thailand. It then carries on to Vietnam and enters the South China Sea south of Ho Chi Minh City. The Mekong is the nation's lifeblood. The river irrigates the rice fields and yields abundant fish. In a country where the roads are difficult to navigate, it also serves as the main thoroughfare—at some point you'll almost inevitably find yourself sailing on the Mekong or one of its many scenic tributaries.

The People

For all the trials and tribulations of their recent history, you won't find a friendlier or more hospitable people than the Lao. Although their language, which is related to Thai, will probably defeat you, one word you're sure to pick up quickly is *Sabaidee*—"welcome" or "hello", and always accompanied by a smile.

Yet it's easy to get a mistaken impression about the cultural and ethnic unity of Laos. Visitors generally see only the people of the plains and the towns. In fact, just half the population are Lao Lum, lowland or valley Lao, originally Tai migrants from southern China. The rest is made up of a patchwork of over 60 ethnic minorities, many of them living in the mountainous regions away from the main cities: the Lao Theung, or mountain Lao, of Indonesian origin and who live on mid-altitude slopes; the Lao Sung, or upland Lao; the Sino-Tibetan Hmong and Yao, and many others.

Most Lao and some of the ethnic groups practice Theravada Buddhism—while many of the more remote hill people remain animists, or spirit worshippers. In the days of the monarchy, these groups formed a complex system of chiefdoms which recognized, more or less, the superiority of the king of Luang Prabang. More recently, some of the non-Lao groups—notably the Hmong—have rigorously resisted the Socialist government in Vientiane and continue to be a troublesome thorn in its side. How the Lao deal with their fellow-countrymen in the hills will be a test of whether or not their laid-back approach to life can be sustained in the years to come.

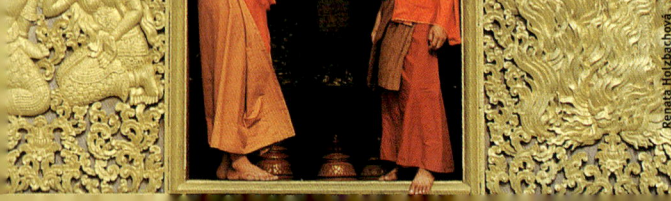

The amazing gold Wat Xieng Thong in Luang Prabang was built by King Setthathirat in the 16th century.

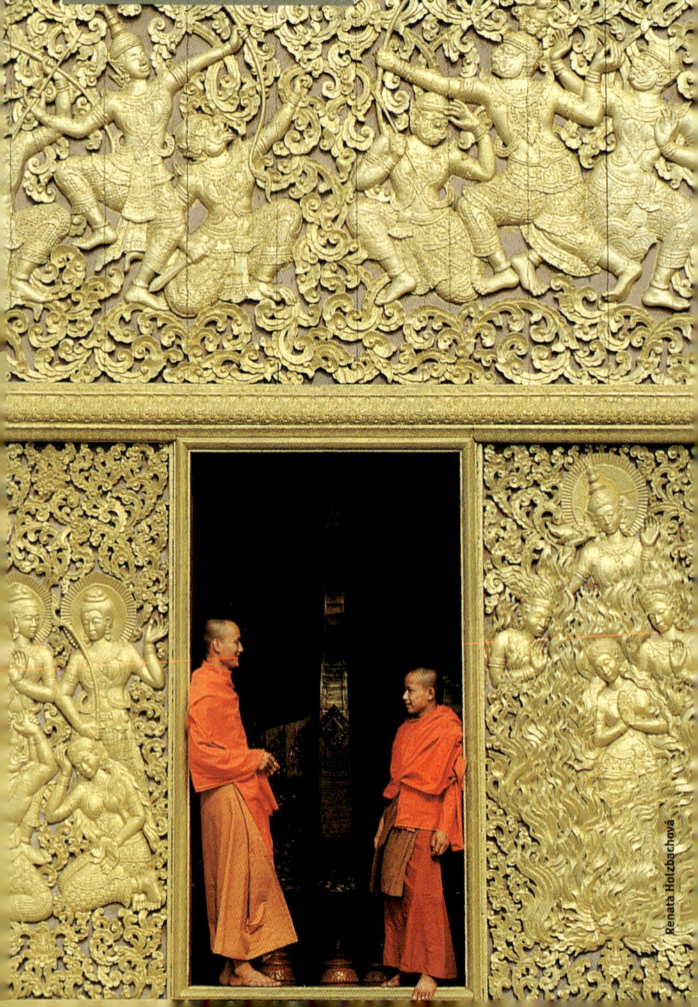

Renata Holzbachová

FLASHBACK

The history of Laos has been profoundly influenced by the actions and ambitions of neighbouring countries. From the 5th century, it was inhabited by a group of tribes known as the Kha, who were under the suzerainty of Funan, a powerful Hindu-Buddhist state based in what is now southern Cambodia and Vietnam.

Some time around the 8th century, the Kha began to be supplanted by the Lao, a Tai-speaking branch of the tribes that controlled the kingdom of Nanchao in southwestern China. They soon established their own principalities and absorbed the local élites.

The Khmers

Throughout this period, Laos continued to be dominated by the great Khmer kingdom of Angkor, which had risen in northern Cambodia in the 9th century and reached its zenith in the 12th century. The Champasak province in the far south of Laos was part of the Angkorian empire itself, and retains important buildings from that time.

Two vital changes came in the 13th century. Lao migration from China, which had been steadily rising over the years, rapidly increased when the Mongols under Kublai Khan destroyed Nanchao. And, as the Angkorian empire began to wane, Lao rulers had to face up to the new geopolitical reality in Indochina and pay tribute to the Siamese to the west. The fast-fading Khmers of Angkor had one last contribution to make to Lao history. In the mid-14th century they equipped the legendary Lao prince, Fa Ngum, with an army and sent him off to conquer the country.

Triumph of Fa Ngum

Nowadays, Fa Ngum is revered by Laotians as the founder of the nation. He had left Laos when young and was educated at the royal court in Angkor, later marrying the king's daughter. In 1351, he led his Khmer army into Laos from the top of a war-elephant. Two years later he fought his way to Muong Swa (now Luang Prabang) where he claimed the throne. He called the

new kingdom Lan Xang and introduced Theravada Buddhism, which was the state religion in Angkor. The warrior-king didn't stop there. For the next 20 years, Fa Ngum kept up a series of conquests, uniting all the Lao principalities in the process, and pushing his empire into northern and eastern Thailand.

Peace and War

Fa Ngum died in 1373, and his successors enjoyed 150 years of relative peace in which to establish the political order of Lan Xang. But the accession to the throne of Photisarath in 1520 marked a turn in the kingdom's fortunes. The ambition of Photisarath was to be a warrior-king in the mould of the great Fa Ngum, and he involved Lan Xang in a number of wars against Burma and the Thai kingdom of Ayutthaya. His aggressive policies managed to see his son placed on the throne of Chiang Mai in 1546, marking Lan Xang's furthest territorial expansion. But this imperial glory was short-lived. The king died two years later in an elephant-riding accident, and

Grottoes by the Mekong have been transformed into shrines. | Khmer-style frieze at Wat Phu, to the south of Pakse. | Farmers of the Lao Sung upland tribe.

his son rushed back to rule as Setthathirat I, leaving Chiang Mai to be rapidly taken over by the Burmese. Lan Xang found itself on the defensive and soon under attack from its neighbours. Fearing the onslaught of the Burmese, Setthathirat moved the capital from Luang Prabang to Vien Chan (now Vientiane) in 1563. The new capital was sacked twice in the next few years, and after the king's death in 1571, the Burmese conquered Vientiane. The kingdom was to remain in a state of chaos well into the next century.

The Lao Golden Age

From this grave position, the nation was about to enter its golden age. This was due primarily to the long reign and charismatic leadership of a new king, Souligna Vongsa, who ascended the throne in 1637 and remained in power for almost 60 years. A soldier, diplomat and patron of the arts, he fought successful wars against rebellious principalities, concluded peace treaties with Siam and Vietnam, and turned Vientiane into an important centre of Buddhist thought.

Division and Foreign Rule

When the king died in 1694, squabbles broke out over the succession. One of his nephews seized the throne with the backing of a Vietnamese army. In response, other members of the royal family, resentful of Vietnamese intrusion, established a separate kingdom in the old capital at Luang Prabang. Then in 1713, another kingdom was formed at Champasak in the south. The country was split into three, and the kingdom of Lan Xang effectively ceased to exist. Weakened and divided, the Lao became easy prey for larger neighbours, and during the 18th century the three kingdoms were annexed by Siam. The Lao kings were permitted to remain in place, but were no more than puppet rulers. So when King Anouvong thought himself strong enough to throw off the Siamese yoke and headed an army against Bangkok in 1827, it only led to the destruction of Vientiane a year later, and saw the region turned into a province of Siam.

Arrival of the French

Paradoxically, the territorial integrity of Laos was restored by the advent of another foreign conqueror in Indochina. France had concluded a first treaty with Vietnam in 1862, and so when the Siamese extended their military control of Laos towards the Vietnamese border, the French protested. It only took the threat of a showdown with the French to make the Siamese withdraw. In

1893, they sent a naval expedition to Bangkok, after which the frontier between Siam and French Indochina was established as the land east of the Mekong River – present-day Laos.

By 1904, the French had completed the annexation of the entire country, locating the administrative centre in Vientiane and allowing the monarch at Luang Prabang to keep his throne under the authority of a French resident supervisor.

Laos remained something of a colonial backwater until World War II, when in March 1945 the Japanese Army took full control from the wartime Vichy government. In response, the first Lao nationalist groups developed, and the nation was about to be transformed once again.

Independent Kingdom

Following the defeat of the Japanese, the French re-occupied the region and attempted to restore the old order. Hoping to marginalize the nationalist Lao Issara (Free Laos) movement, they set up King Sisavang Vong of Luang Prabang as the nominal ruler of a unified Laos within the French Union. But a new and more radical nationalism soon emerged. The Pathet Lao was created in 1950 under the leadership of Kaysone Phomvihan and Prince Souphanouvong, who was nicknamed the Red Prince in the West. They sided with the Vietminh against the French and gained power in northeast Laos. In the face of major military setbacks in the region, France finally withdrew from Indochina in 1954, and Laos became an independent kingdom.

Civil War

Throughout this time, the king's claim to represent a united nation was on shaky ground, as Pathet Lao forces continued to hold the northeastern provinces. The fragile peace ended in 1959 when civil war broke out between the Pathet Lao and the royal government. There was a temporary respite in 1962 during a short-lived coalition government that included both sides. But when the civil war got under way again two years later, it was as part of the greater regional conflict of the Vietnam War. The famous Ho Chi Minh Trail, running through northern Laos and used as a supply line by the North Vietnamese, became the target of US bombing raids; more than 2 million tonnes of explosives were dropped on eastern Laos in the years up to the end of the war.

Pathet Lao Seize Power

When the North Vietnamese defeated the US and marched into Saigon in April 1975, they began a chain-reaction of other communist takeovers in Indochina. The Khmer Rouge took control in Cambodia that same month, and shortly afterwards, in a bloodless coup, the Pathet Lao proclaimed the Lao People's Democratic Republic under President Souphanouvong—and the 600-year-old Lao monarchy was abolished.

Laos today

After the coup, the new government imitated the Vietnamese economic model and established a programme of collectivization in the countryside, nationalization of industry, and "re-education" camps for members of the former Lao military and political elite. As a consequence, up to 10 per cent of the population fled to Thailand. The Lao economy suffered dramatically, and so in 1980 private ownership was re-introduced. The links with Vietnam and the Soviet Union loosened after the end of the cold war in the late 1980s, and the building and development projects that are being carried out today are more likely to be funded by Japan, Australia and the international agencies. A new constitution enacted in 1991 permitted Laotians far greater freedom of movement at home and abroad.

The country is still one of the poorest in Asia and continues to be blighted by a vast quantity of unexploded bombs dropped by the Americans in the Vietnam War. But with Thailand now its main trading partner, and having secured membership of the Association of South-East Asia Nations (ASEAN) in 1997, Laos has begun to shake off its sense of isolation and looks to a future that's increasingly open to the world. Tourist numbers are gradually increasing, and it is planned to extend Laos's first railway—a 3.5-km link over the Thai-Lao Friendship Bridge—a further 10 km to Vientiane.

King Sisavang Vong was a lifetime supporter of French rule.

Pra That Luang, the Great Sacred Stupa, and King Settathirat who built it.

ON THE SCENE

Vientiane can be used as a base for side trips to places such as the great statue park of Xiang Khuan, while the Pak Ou Caves and their myriad Buddhas can be visited from Luang Prabang. Not to be missed is the mysterious Plain of Jars. For a taste of Laos at its most remote, and a glimpse of its fascinating hill tribes, it's worth trying to reach one or two of the outlying provinces, while in Champasak, in the far south, the ruins of the greatest Khmer temple outside Cambodia are sure to impress.

Vientiane

Vientiane has been the capital of Laos since the 16th century. The city developed at the point where the first navigable reach of the Mekong flows out of the mountains and intersects with the road linking southern China and the Gulf of Thailand. It came under Siamese control in the 18th century, and was sacked in 1828 and the inhabitants deported. Many of its finest temples were destroyed, and little of what you see today predates the Siamese invasion. The city was still deserted when the French arrived in the 1860s, and it was under French colonial rule that restoration work was carried out on important buildings such as That Luang.

Over the last few years, Vientiane has become a city of internet cafés, tourist hotels and international restaurants. Amazingly, this has happened without the place losing its laid-back and uniquely Lao character.

City Centre
Built on a curve of the Mekong, the city centre has a grid-plan layout, with the river to the south and Nam Phu Place in the centre. It's very compact and easy to walk around, with plenty of pleasant bars and cafés.

Nam Phu Place
Though it's not exactly a Piccadilly Circus or Time Square, Nam Phu Place is as close to being a downtown hub as you're likely to

find in Vientiane. It's marked by a fountain in the centre, while nearby are restaurants, a Scandinavian bakery, tourist agencies and hotels.

At the south end runs Setthathirat Road, a delightful tree-lined boulevard which contains some of the city's finest temples.

Lao National Museum

In a French colonial dwelling on Samsenthai Road north of Nam Phu Place, once used for government offices, this used to be known as the Lao Revolutionary Museum. The old name tells you much about the displays inside. A few rooms take in archaeological finds, anthropological information on Laos's ethnic groups and the history of the kingdom of Lan Xang, but the bulk of the museum is devoted to artefacts and photos documenting the Pathet Lao's struggle for power against the French, the Americans and the royalist government. In this light, it's a fascinating relic from the Cold War era, where you can see items such as Comrade Souphanouvong's table, at which the Red Prince developed his plans to create a revolution, or photos and paintings captioned with suitably anti-Western propaganda. There's also a small but interesting display of Lao produce, crafts and manufactured goods.

The Wat. It's not simply a temple or a monastery. A wat is at once a place of worship, a school, a hospital and a meeting place. All wats are built on the same pattern. Between the outer and inner walls are the monks' dormitories *(kutis)*, a belltower *(ho rakang)* and a library *(ho trai)*, where Buddhist scriptures are stored. The inner wall separates the sacred and the profane, and often takes the form of a cloister lined with images of Buddha, to encourage meditation. In the courtyard, the rectangular *viharn* is an assembly hall. Reserved for the monks, the temple, *sim*, houses the main image of Buddha. The *sim* itself is surrounded by stone tablets, or boundary markers, placed at the principal and intermediate points of the compass. A number of chambers *(that)*, in the form of lotus buds, contain holy relics of Buddha or the ashes of royalty, dignitaries or monks. Some wats also have a *ho phi khun*, or spirit house, for the temple's reigning earth spirit. Though the worship of spirits has been banned, the Lao still make offerings to these guardians of people or places.

Presidential Palace and Colonial Quarter

Follow Setthathirat Road eastwards from Nam Phu Place and you'll come to the colonial splendour of the Presidential Palace. It stands on the site of the former royal palace, and was occupied in succession by the French Resident during the protectorate, the king of reunified Laos, and latterly the president of the Lao Republic.

The administrative part of town huddles around the palace. Just beyond it is the old colonial quarter, with several other buildings dating from the time of the French Protectorate. In particular, look out for the cathedral, the hospital and the French embassy, all of which give some idea of the colonial style of architecture that the French brought to Indochina.

Antique head of Buddha displayed in Wat Si Saket; the wall behind is riddled with niches to hold smaller images.

Wat Ho Pra Keo

Next door, this temple was the chapel of the royal palace. It was restored by prince Souvanna Phouma and transformed into a remarkable museum of religious art. The chapel was built during the 1560s to shelter the Pra Keo, or Emerald Buddha, but this was carried off by the Siamese in 1778 and is still held in Bangkok. Apart from the fabulous sculpted doors and golden throne, you'll see an impressive collection of Buddhas going back to the 6th century. Images of Buddha are always carved in stylized postures called *mudra*. The "Calling for Rain" posture is typically Lao; it depicts the Buddha standing with his hands held rigidly at each side, fingers pointing to the ground.

Look out too for an 18th-century throne in the form of a *naga*, a mythical serpent. In the garden is one of the famous great stone jars, transported by helicopter from the Plain of Jars.

Wat Si Saket

Opposite the Presidential Palace, this is the residence of the Buddhist community, Pra Sangka Nagnok. It was built in 1818 by King Anouvong and spared from destruction in the Siamese attack ten years later, possibly because it was designed in a Siamese architectural style.

The interior walls of the cloister are packed with hundreds of Buddhas in all sizes and of all materials, in small niches and on shelves in front of them. In the main sanctuary (*sim*) note the outstanding Naga Buddha in Khmer style, seated beneath a canopy formed by a multi-headed *naga*, and the 19th-century murals depicting episodes from the reincarnated lives of the Buddha. The coffered ceiling is decorated with a floral motif inspired by the Thai temples of Ayutthaya. Behind the *sim*, a long wooden trough sculpted in the form of a *naga* serves at New Year when the images of Buddha are sprinkled with holy water for ritual cleansing.

Wat Si Muang

Further east along Setthathirat Road, the lower town still retains something of a village atmosphere. The heart of this area is dominated by Wat Si Muang, at the main crossroads. This is the site of the city pillar, *lak muang*, and is thus considered the home of Vientiane's guardian spirit. According to legend, when the hole was dug for the pillar, a pregnant girl jumped in and the ropes were released, her sacrifice establishing the town guardianship. Today, it's a bright, bustling temple, with a continual stream of worshippers from the local community, and numerous street stalls outside selling saffron, candles and other items to make up offerings to the shrine.

Wat Ong Teu

Head back towards the stretch of Setthathirat Road west of Nam Phu Place, with its string of attractive monasteries. Surrounded by the residences of high-ranking families and set in a delightful garden, Wat Ong Teu is known for its enormous bronze Buddha. Cast in the 16th century, the statue weighs several tons—indeed, Wat Ong Teu means the "Temple of the Heavy Buddha". This is an especially lively place to be in November when the That Luang festival is celebrated here, dating from the times when the nobles swore allegiance to the king and constitution.

Along the Mekong River

Follow any street south from the city centre and you come to Fa Ngum Road, which runs alongside the Mekong. The riverside here provides a pleasant place for a late-afternoon stroll. It also has great sunset views and is lined with bars and foodstalls at which to enjoy them.

Around Vientiane
A new and more expansive town has sprung up outside the ancient fortifications. Unless you're a dedicated city-walker you will probably want to take a taxi from the centre to places such as the Patuxai arch and the historic That Luang temple.

Lan Xang Avenue
Leading from the Presidential Palace up to a large triumphal arch, this wide boulevard self-consciously evokes the Champs-Elysées in Paris, though it's certainly a fairly run-down version. Here you'll find banks, the main post office, the tourist information bureau and the Morning Market, known as Talat Sao. This vast affair is surprisingly hassle-free compared to most South-East Asian markets, and is filled with stalls selling jewellery, textiles, clothes, electronic goods and souvenirs.

Patuxai Arch
At the top of Lan Xang Avenue, the Patuxai, also called Anusavari ("Monument") is a triumphal arch built to commemorate the Lao who died in the pre-Revolu-

Twilight over the calm waters of the Mekong.

tionary wars. Though inspired by the Arc de Triomphe in Paris, it incorporates Lao architectural and decorative motifs. Work began on it in 1958, and it's said to have been completed using concrete initially intended by the Americans for expanding the airport—locals have nicknamed it the "vertical runway". For good views of the city, you can climb the stairway to the top.

Pra That Luang
A 15-minute walk east of Patuxai, the Great Sacred Stupa is the

A pagoda hidden away in the forest near Vang Vieng.

national place of pilgrimage, the most venerated Buddhist monument in the country. Built by King Setthathirat in 1566 on the site of a Khmer temple, it was restored by a French university department in the 1930s. In ritual worship, the faithful make their way along the two terraces, from left to right, to reach the golden stupa, crowned by a spire in the form of an elongated lotus bud. During the fierce daytime sunlight the stupa is almost too dazzling to look at, and is seen to best effect at sunset or at the time of the That Luang Festival, of which this shrine is the focus.

Beyond the City

Outside the capital there are several interesting places to visit, ranging from the eccentricities of a Buddhist theme park to the atmospheric karst caves in the Lao countryside around Vang Vieng. The bus journey takes 3 to 4 hours; buses leave every hour till 3 p.m. from the station near the market in Vientiane.

Suan Vathanatham

Located 20 km (12 miles) downstream of Vientiane, the National Ethnic Culture Park contains a rich assortment of attractions, including replicas of traditional Lao houses, concrete dinosaurs, a small zoo, bars, restaurants and views of the Friendship Bridge.

Wat Xieng Khuan

A further 4 km (2.5 miles) away, Wat Xieng Khuan is not really a wat. Created in the 1950s and 60s by a monk, Luang Pu Bunleua Sulilat, it's a sort of mystical garden cum religious theme park, planted with a bizarre assortment of cement sculptures representing various divinities that include Shiva, Vishnu and Buddha. You can get an overview of the park by climbing to the top of a large structure that's meant to represent the three levels of existence—hell, earth and heaven. It's undoubtedly unusual and all rather kitsch. In case you're moved to wonder about the park's creator, Luang Pu fled to Thailand after the Pathet Lao came to power, and built another one there.

Vang Vieng

A small town 156 km (97 miles) north of Vientiane, Vang Vieng is scenically located on the banks of the Nam Xong river. It's set among limestone karst hills perforated by a series of caves. The best-known and most accessible of these is **Tham Chang**, where you can see intriguing rock formations, swim in a stream and enjoy great views over the valley from its mouth. The caves a little further out, such as **Tham Phu Kam** and **Tham Xang** offer spectacular karst scenery and a dramatic sense of isolation.

Resplendent in red and gold, Wat Mai is the most important temple of Luang Prabang.

Luang Prabang

The former royal capital is a small town surrounded by lush, green mountains, where the Khan river flows into the Mekong. It has been at the heart of Lao culture ever since Fa Ngum established it as the capital of Lan Xang in 1353

Known for the next two centuries by its original name of Muong Swa, it acquired its current name under King Setthathirat in 1563 in honour of the Pra Bang, a gold Buddha made in Sri Lanka and brought here by Fa Ngum from Angkor. That same year, the king relocated the capital to Vientiane. The town had a new lease of life as a royal capital in 1707, when Lan Xang disintegrated and the kingdom of Luang Prabang emerged. A proud tradition of Lao music and dance, architecture, craftsmanship and haute cuisine grew up around the court. Although the royal connection ended with the Pathet Lao revolution of 1975, the city remains a fascinating compendium of traditional Lao culture, both sacred and profane.

The Old City
The old city of Luang Prabang is enclosed in a curve traced by the Nam Khan, the northern part forming a long peninsula. In the centre is a large hill, the Phu Si, a symbol of a cosmic mountain emerging from the waters. Around this is the magnificent royal palace, a host of beautiful sloping-roof temples, and numerous ancient lanes and alleyways. Be sure to get out by 6 a.m. on at least one morning, when you'll find rows of saffron-robed monks silently collecting alms. Certainly, it's a place rich in atmosphere, and steeped in the history of the country's glorious past.

Royal Palace
Located between Phu Si hill and the Mekong, the former Royal Palace was rebuilt by the French as a permanent structure in 1904, during the reign of King Sisavang Vong, and topped by a graceful Lao-style spire a quarter of a century later. It's made up of three embedded parts: the reception rooms, the throne room, and the private chambers. The palace was converted into a museum in 1976, a year after the last king of Laos was sent into exile.

The collections include classical instruments, masks used for performances of the *Ramayana*, paintings of Luang Prabang executed by the French artist Alix de Fautereau in 1930, numerous religious objects and mementoes of the monarchy. There's also a room devoted to the diplomatic gifts presented to Laos. The most prized work of art in the museum is the Pra Bang, a small standing statue of the Buddha said to be made of solid gold, and which gave its name to the city. It's kept in a purpose-built shrine near the entrance to the palace, and is said by some to be a copy, with the original stored away in a bank vault.

Wat Mai

Next to the palace, Wat Mai (or Wat Mai Suvannaphumaham, to give it its full name) was the residence of the Sangkhalat, the highest dignitary of the Lao Buddhist church. The temple dates from the late 18th century, and serves as a chapel for the palace. During the lively New Year celebrations it becomes the scene of a ritual baptism of the Pra Bang. On the front veranda, the superb gold relief door panels tell the story of Pra Wet, the penultimate reincarnation of Buddha.

Night Market

Every evening from 5 p.m., the stretch of road in front of the Royal Palace closes to traffic and is taken over by the few hundred stalls of the Handicraft Night Market. This started as a Christmas market in 2002 and has never looked back. There is no hard-sell in this quiet market; you will find a wealth of crafts ranging from silk scarves to chess sets. It is customary to bargain, but the prices are very low anyway. More and more goods from China and Vietnam are sold here, in addition to products made by the local Hmong who started the market.

Phu Si

Opposite the Royal Palace is the Phu Si hill. You can climb up the 328 steps to the top, where you'll be rewarded with great views of the town, as well as the rivers and jungle-covered mountains that surround it. This is also a very popular place at sunset. The hill was covered in temples in the 18th century, but there are only five left. That Chom Si, built in 1804 crowns the summit, and is the starting-point for the torch-lit procession at Lao New Year in April.

Wat Aham and Wat Visun

Behind Phu Si, away from the main part of town, are some stunning views of the Khan river and the hills beyond. If you continue on the road south, keeping the Nam Khan on your left, you'll come to two of the city's finest temples.

Wat Aham encloses the shrine of the royal spirit protector, Ho Phi Khon, at the base of two large bodhi trees. Immediately next to it, Wat Visun is renowned for its collection of religious art which includes a number of Buddhas in the "Calling for Rain" posture.

The original wooden temple was built in 1512, but marauding Chinese Ho burned it to the ground in 1887.

In front of the temple, **That Pathum**, the Lotus Stupa, is built in the shape of a watermelon. Also known as That Makmo, the 34.5-m (113-ft) structure was built by order of Nang Phantin Xieng, wife of King Visun, at the beginning of the 16th century. The stupa's unusual shape recalls the mythological origins of the Lao culture: the legend recounts that a certain Khun Borom cut open a gourd somewhere near Dien Bien Phu (in Vietnam) and out sprang seven sons who spread the Thai-Lao family east and west.

Wat Xieng Thong

Near the tip of the peninsula, overlooking the Mekong, the magnificent Wat Xieng Thong was the city's most important royal temple and ranks as one of the richest artistic achievements in Laos. It was built by King Setthathirat in 1560. The *sim* is in classic Luang Prabang style, with a stunning tiered roof and gilt murals on its black exterior walls. Enter through decorated doors to the dark interior, whose columns, beams and walls are covered in superb gold-leaf murals.

Just behind the *sim* is a small shrine with a striking mosaic design and a standing Buddha inside. Look out too for the Red Chapel, with its highly regarded sculpture of a reclining Buddha.

Across the courtyard is the modern Funerary Carriage Hall, containing the royal funeral carriages and urns, together with a small collection of puppets, currency and other mementoes from the royalist era.

Wat Pakkhan

Not far from Wat Xieng Thong, this temple is close to the mouth of the Nam Khan; the king used to watch the royal regattas from its platform. Dating from the 18th century, its handsome doors reveal a Chinese influence.

The Lower Town

Lesser mortals lived—and still do—in the lower town, where you'll discover the markets and countless artisans, with the silversmiths bunched together down by the river. The district boasts some of the city's oldest and finest temples—Buddhism was late coming to Luang Prabang and at first was restricted to this area.

Wat That, or Wat Pra Mahathat, sits at the top of a staircase with a *naga* balustrade and has some outstanding woodcarvings on the façade.

Further out, **Wat That Luang** was built at the beginning of the 19th century and contains the ashes of members of the royal family. The gold stupa at one end of the compound is the mausoleum of the last king of Laos.

Around Luang Prabang
There are some intriguing places of interest close to the city. They can be easily reached either by road or scenic Mekong river boat rides.

Across the Mekong
Plenty of ferries are on hand to take you across the river. On the riverbank, **Wat Long Khun** is where each new king of Luang Prabang would spend a three-day retreat before his coronation. The red, blue and gold carved doors of the temple are especially noteworthy.

Not far from here, **Wat Tham** is located inside a cave 100-m (328 ft) deep. It contains vast quantities of old Buddhas, though it isn't lit, so you'll need to bring a torch if you want to see anything. Climb the path to **Wat Chom Phet**. The temple is no longer in use and there are tales of spirits haunting the place — but it also offers unparalleled sunset views of Luang Prabang.

Pak Ou Caves
Boats can be hired from the pier in front of the Royal Palace to the caves, about 25 km (15 miles) upstream along the Mekong. The setting is delightful in itself but also holds symbolic interest. In a triple-peak mountain landscape at the confluence of the Mekong and the Ou, two caves — **Tham Thing** and **Tham Phum** — burrow into a limestone cliff. They represent the womb of the earth, out of which trickle the first waters of life, irrigating and purifying the land. These caves are particularly revered by the Lao, as you can see from the offerings of thousands of Buddhas that have accumulated over the centuries.

Kuang Si Waterfall
Located about 30 km (18 miles) to the west of Luang Prabang, these picturesque falls are a great place to avoid the midday heat. With a 60-m (196-ft) drop over jutting rocks, the spray keeps the area refreshingly cool, and there are also plenty of small pools that are delightful for swimming. Bear in mind that this is a popular weekend picnic spot with the locals and can get very crowded; during the week you'll find it a haven of peace. The falls can be reached by river or road. This last route allows you to see villages inhabited by ethnic groups such as the Hmong and Lao Theung.

Plain of Jars
This vast, mysterious plain in Xieng Khuang Province, 12 km (7 miles) south of Phonsavan, is scattered with hundreds of huge

stone jars gaping towards the heavens. In varying sizes, they measure up to 2.5 m (8 ft) tall, and the biggest weighs a hefty 6 tons. Here and there lie big stone lids. Adding to the mystery is the fact that the stone was not quarried locally, and no one knows how it was transported here. Moreover, tools and bronze ornaments were discovered in this area, left by a civilization that has not yet been identified — some anthropologists believe they are the traces of a lost Indochinese people. A number of different theories have been proposed as to the purpose of these jars: perhaps they were sarcophagi, or maybe they were used for storing grain or fermenting wine.

When you go exploring, do not stray too far off the main paths without a reliable guide. During the Vietnam War, this area was fought over by government forces, Pathet Lao insurgents and North Vietnamese troops, as well as being intensively bombed by the Americans. There's still a considerable amount of unexploded ordnance here. Miraculously, however, most of the jars escaped damage.

One of the world's mysteries: the stone receptacles of the Plain of Jars. | **Buddha in the Pak Ou Caves.**

The twin waterfalls of Tad Fan on the Bolaven Plateau.

The South

On the banks of the Mekong, Savannakhet stands at the crossroads of road 13 to the far south, and road 9 eastwards to Vietnam.

Savannakhet
Commonly known as Savan, the town was founded by the French and has an attractive colonial quarter around the town square. The shrine of the city's guardian spirit looks out over the river, but the main temple, **Wat Sayaphum**, stands on the landward side of the road running along the river bank, sheltering the municipality's ceremonial boat.

In an old colonial mansion, the **provincial museum** has displays on local boy Kaysone Phomvihan, one of the founders of Pathet Lao, and relics dating from the time of the Vietnam War.

That Ing Hang
At the village of Ban That, north of Savan, That Ing Hang is of Khmer inspiration; it is considered to be the holiest religious building in southern Laos. Three superimposed terraces are topped by the traditional Lao stupa and a gold umbrella. Many of the sculptures are erotic, recalling one of the symbolic meanings of the stupa: the image of a phallus reaching towards the fecund heavens.

Champasak Province
After the Khemmarat rapids, the Mekong flows peacefully for 200 km (120 miles) before tumbling into the Khon Phapheng Falls. The basin forms a distinctive region with a complicated history. It was part of the Angkor empire from the 10th to the 13th centuries, then was incorporated into the Lan Xang kingdom, breaking away to become the autonomous principality of Champasak in 1713. Parts were whittled away by Siam, and the remainder was integrated into French Indochina, though the people remained faithful to the local monarchy. In 1946, when Laos was reunified, the crown prince Boun Oum renounced his rights to the throne, but he was able to maintain the ritual and symbolic apparatus of his ancestry. Until the Communists took power. The prince fled to Paris, where he died in 1980.

Pakse
The bustling regional capital lies at the confluence of the Mekong and the Xe Don. Prince Boun Oum started building a five-storey palace here in 1968 but never had time to finish it. It has now been converted into a hotel. You might also want to check out the **provincial museum**, which has interesting examples of Khmer art as well as jewellery and cos-

tumes from Laos's ethnic groups, alongside the inevitable displays devoted to the triumph of the Pathet Lao revolution.

Ban Saphai

A short distance from Pakse on the west bank of the Mekong, Ban Saphai village is well known for maintaining traditional hand-weaving techniques. You can watch the weavers work at their looms, and purchase the silk textiles they produce here.

Bolaven Plateau

This high plateau to the east of Pakse provides relief from the heat of the Mekong valley. Its fertile red soil, of volcanic origin, has been farmed intensively since the French first introduced coffee, rubber and bananas in the early 20th century. Now strawberries and raspberries, cardamom and rattan are also grown here. The main town, Paksong, was virtually destroyed in the war.

The Bolaven plateau and the area of Saravan to the north are home to a score of Mon-Khmer minority groups, including the Alak, Taoy, Tahok, Suay and Katu. Treks to their villages are a great way of seeing the countryside; buses run to places such as the spectacular Tad Lo and Tad Fan waterfalls.

Wat Phu

On the right bank of the Mekong, 30 km (18 miles) south of Pakse, is a mountain shaped like an immense *lingam*, the phallic symbol of Shiva. The site of the temple at its foot has been sacred since prehistoric times. The present temple is of Khmer origin — possibly dating originally from the pre-Angkorian era of the 5th or 6th century, but completed by Suryavarman II, the 12th-century

> **The Baci.** For important events in family life (before a long journey, after serious illness, a birth, a marriage, a homecoming and so on), the Lao hold a ceremony called the *baci,* or *sukwan*, thus upholding an animist tradition. Before noon or sunset, the neighbours are invited to gather around a tray laden with fruit, eggs, sweetmeats and flowers, arranged in the form of a cosmic mountain. From it dangle 32 cotton strings. A village elder recites a prayer to summon the 32 *kwan*, the guardian spirits that each watch over the different organs of a person's body. Once the wandering *kwan* have returned to the body, the guests tie the strings round their wrists to retain them, and make wishes. The offerings are shared out, then the dancing and merry-making can begin. The threads should be worn for three days.

king who built the great Angkor Wat in northern Cambodia.

It is built on megalithic terraces from the 1st millennium BC. The three main levels are linked by a processional causeway which would once have been flanked by statues of lions and mythical beasts. On the uppermost level, the main sanctuary once housed a large lingam that was washed by water channelled from the holy spring flowing from a cave at the top of the hill. Here, the views over the ancient temple complex and the mysterious jungle that encloses it are breathtaking.

Khon Phapheng Falls

Near the Cambodian border, the Mekong breaks up into a tangle of channels and waterfalls, forming hundreds of islands. In a 13-km (8-mile) stretch of powerful rapids, the Khon Phapheng falls, 160 km (100 miles) downstream from Pakse, are just 15 m (49 ft) high but the largest cascades by water volume in all South-East Asia. There's a wooden pavilion on the riverbank for viewing them: the bamboo scaffolding on the rocks is used by local fishermen who benefit from divine protection by the spirits of the falls.

Deftly weaving baskets. | **A banana flower.** | **Main stairway leading up to the temple of Wat Phu.**

If you want to keep cool, buy a parasol—something easy to carry home.

SHOPPING

Once you have brushed aside the tourist trash, you'll discover that Laos is a nation of skilled craftsmen, producing great-value handcrafted goods using materials such as textiles and silver.

If you're travelling beyond the main cities, you can buy locally made items in the villages themselves or at provincial markets. Otherwise, scout around Vientiane's vast Morning Market or the Dala Market in Luang Prabang for a wide range of Laotian handicrafts. Luang Prabang also has a popular night market, selling crafts made by local Hmong people.

Textiles
Rough-textured fabrics of silk or cotton are a Lao speciality. The dominant colour is navy, interwoven with traditional designs whose origins are lost in the mists of time. Every ethnic group, every province has its distinctive patterns. In general, the lengths are made up in standard sizes for a skirt (*sin*) or a scarf, wall hangings or bed covers.

There's also a tradition of "aristocratic" weaving: a smooth silk intended for clothes worn for ceremonious occasions or going to the temple. These fabrics are lighter in colour, in faded or pastel tones, sometimes shot through with gold threads. Particular attention is paid to the strip forming the hem of the *sin*.

Silverware
Lao jewellery is generally made of silver and sold by weight. It is divided into two styles: that of the hill tribes and that of the plains. You'll see belts, bracelets, anklets and necklaces on show. There are also silverware items like decorated boxes and bowls, as well as animal and human figures. With a bit of patience you can find articles of exceptional purity and beauty, especially in Luang Prabang, where the tradition of the royal silversmiths has managed to survive the end of the monarchy.

Other handicrafts
Wooden objects can range from sculpted images of the Buddha to ornately carved pipes. Traditional village craftsmen favour materials like rattan, wicker and bamboo for utensils, mats and furniture.

DINING OUT

Closer in spirit to Thai rather than Chinese or Vietnamese cooking, the distinctive taste of Lao cuisine is created with flavours such as lime juice, fresh coriander, lemon grass, chillies and fermented fish sauces. Main ingredients include chicken, beef and pork, although the favoured traditional food is freshwater fish.

Home Cooking

Lao cuisine is frequently fiery and always piquant, so the perfect accompaniment is rice and a glass of excellent Lao-brewed beer. However, there are not many Lao restaurants—Chinese and Vietnamese establishments are in far greater supply. It's often said that to find the best Lao food you have to be invited to someone's home. European and American cuisine is well represented in the main cities these days, with some first-rate French cooking now to be found in Vientiane and Luang Prabang.

The Basics

The Lao are rice eaters. The grain is a particularly appetizing variety, improperly known as glutinous, or sticky rice, *khao nio*. It does not grow in great quantity, but is very nutritious. To prepare it, the rice is soaked for several hours, then steamed and served in little baskets. You take up a portion with four fingers and form it into a little ball, which you dip into the accompanying dishes.

Rice is generally served with *padek*, a pungent concoction of fish macerated in wheat germ and salt. *Kin khao kap padek*, literally "to eat sticky rice and padek", is the staple peasant meal.

The other staple guaranteed to gladden the heart of any Lao is noodles, mainly eaten for breakfast in a spicy broth called *foe*. You'll also come across *khao pun*, which is an extremely popular noodle dish served with an assortment of raw vegetables and seasoned with a meat, fish and coconut sauce; and a chicken-and-ginger version, *khao biak sen*. These are best enjoyed at street stalls and noodle shops.

Main courses

A serious contender for the title of Lao national dish, *laap* is a banquet meal of minced raw beef or venison mixed with aubergine, chilli, fish sauce, garlic and shallots. It's run a close second by green papaya salad, *tam mak houng*: shredded green papaya, chilli, garlic and lime juice.

Soups will be brought with the other main dishes, as they are not considered as starters. Try *gaeng pag nam*, made from watercress; *tom yam pa*, a fish, lemon grass and mushroom soup; or *gaeng jeut*, with pork and vegetables.

Also on the menu might be *goy moo*, pork salad with fresh herbs; *kali kai*, a spicy chicken curry; *phanang-kai*, chicken with peanut stuffing; and *sa ton pa*, raw fish chopped and spiced with a complicated sauce.

A real treat if you're in Luang Prabang is *mok pa*, steamed fish in banana leaves. Other possibilities include *tom-pon* and *o-pa*, both based on boiled fish pepped up with spices; *mu-nem*, minced pork with lettuce; *sin-heng*, dried buffalo or venison; *khua*, meat sautéed with garlic and onions; *roy tium*, fish parcels; and *som khay*, a type of caviar.

For dessert, you might find restaurants offering *ngoon kati*, coconut jelly, or *nam wan mak kuay*, banana in coconut milk. Delicious in the mango season, *khao niaw mak muang* is rice pudding with mango and coconut.

Drinks

The French began growing coffee on the Bolaven Plateau in southern Laos in the early 20th century — the Lao like to take it very strong and very sweet.

Fruit juices and sweetened fruit shakes are popular, and available at street stalls and shops throughout every town.

The Lao's favourite tipple is *lao-lao*, a strong spirit made from rice. Some villages are reputed for the quality of their *lao-lao*, such as the one halfway between Luang Prabang and the Pak Ou Caves. Light in colour, locally brewed Beer Lao is delicious with spicy Lao food.

Renata Holzbachová

THE HARD FACTS

Airports
Wattay International Airport is situated 6 km (4 miles) west of Vientiane; Luang Prabang Airport is a mere 2 km east of the ancient capital. The terminals have cafés, currency exchange and duty-free facilities.

If you do not already have special arrangements made for the journey into town (some hotels offer a free pick-up service), you'll find plenty of taxis outside the terminal buildings.

You will have to pay a departure tax on international and domestic flights.

Climate
Laos has a tropical climate, with a monsoon season bringing heavy rains between May and September, and a dry season from October to April. The coolest period is between November and January, when average temperatures get down to a comfortable 28°C (82°F), though in the highlands it can become very cold indeed at this time; the hottest is April, with temperatures regularly reaching 36°C (96.8°F).

Communications
The postal service in Laos is efficient and reliable. As well as selling stamps and phonecards, the main post offices in Vientiane and Luang Prabang offer telephone, fax and post restante facilities. The post office in Vientiane is on the corner of Khu Vieng Road and Lan Xang Avenue; in Luang Prabang it's right at the main intersection of the old town, near the tourist office.

Laotel phonecards can be purchased from shops and hotels as well as the post office. Two mobile phone operators, Tigo and Laotel, offer roaming services.

The international access code is 00, followed by the country code, 1 for USA and Canada, 44 for UK, 61 for Australia, then the area code (minus initial zero) and the local number. The country code for Laos if you are dialling from abroad is 856; the city code for Vientiane is 021; Luang Prabang is 071.

Faxes can be sent and received at hotels, but are expensive. The Internet is very popular in Laos, and is by far the cheapest way of keeping in touch with people at home. There are plenty of Internet cafés in the main cities, and still easily found elsewhere in the country. Larger hotels also offer this facility. Access can be very slow.

Driving

Foreign tourists are permitted to rent cars and motorbikes. However, given the difficult driving conditions that prevail here, it's usually a more stress-free option as well as less expensive to hire a car with a driver. This will probably be a necessity if you want to get to any out-of-the-way places, as public transport is very slow. Car hire can be arranged through your hotel or a reputable travel agent.

Emergencies

Most problems can be handled at your hotel desk. If you have a medical problem, there are various clinics in Vientiane that can offer an international standard of healthcare. To call an ambulance dial 195.

The Medical Centre of the French Embassy provides health care and paramedical services, including dental treatment, 24 hours a day, 7 days a week, to all French expats and tourists in Vientiane. It is on Khu Vieng Road, tel. 021 214 150.

The Australian Embassy Clinic on Thadeua Road opens Mon–Fri 8.30 a.m.– 12.30 p.m. and 1.30–7 p.m., tel. 021 343840; it accepts Canadian, American and English patients but Australians have preference. There's an International Clinic at the Mahosat Hospital Centre, tel. 021 4022.

As a last resort, emergency transfers by ambulance to the Aek Udon International Hospital in Udon Thani, Thailand, can be arranged; tel. 0066 42 342 555. Ambulances from Setthathirat hospital can also cross the border, tel. 021 351 156. The bridge is open from 6 a.m. to 10 p.m.

Formalities

You will need a passport, valid for at least six months before its expiry date. Tourist visas valid for 30 days are issued on arrival at Vientiane, Luang Prabang and Pakse airports, and cost about US$30. One extension is permitted. You must hold a return or onward ticket and a confirmed hotel reservation in Laos; you also need a passport-size photo of yourself (3 x 4 cm). Embassies of Laos in the US, Australia, France or Germany, among others, can issue visas at varying costs, usually in 2 or 3 days. In the UK, officially recognized tour companies can probably obtain a visa for you.

Health

Before you leave be sure to buy travel insurance that includes medical cover, and have all the necessary immunizations—contact your doctor or travel centre to find out what's required. You'll also need to start taking a course of antimalarial tablets prior to departure. Preventing the insects getting to you is best, though, so it's a good idea to take mosquito repellent, and keep your arms and legs covered in the evenings if possible.

With a little care you should encounter no health problems during your stay. It's wise to avoid too much exposure to the sun. Wear a hat, use a good sunscreen and keep in the shade as much as possible, especially in the middle of the day. Drink plenty of mineral water to avoid dehydration—never tap water. In the same vein, do not eat salad or fruit that has been washed in unpurified water, and beware of ice cubes and fruit juice diluted with tap water—indeed, it's even worth brushing your teeth in mineral water.

If you require specialized prescription medicines, remember to take enough with you to last for the duration of your stay.

Holidays and Festivals

Many of Laos's public holidays and festivals follow the lunar calendar, and so move from year to year. During all of the following public holidays and most of the festivals, you'll find banks and offices shut.

January 1	New Year's Day
January 6	Pathet Lao Day
January 20	Army Day
March 8	International Women's Day
March 22	Lao People's Party Day
May 1	International Labour Day
June 1	International Children's Day
August 13	*Lao Issara* (independence of the Lao people)
October 12	Liberation Day
December 2	National Day (parades and plenty of flag-waving)

Moveable festivals:

Dec–Jan: *Boun Pha Wet* celebrates the penultimate incarnation of the Buddha with music and dancing.

March: *Boun Khoun Khao* is thanksgiving.

Mid-April: *Boun Pimai*, the Lao New Year, is a time of processions and riotous merry-making, like Thailand's Songkran.

May: *Boun Bang Fai* is known as the Rocket Festival: fireworks are fired heavenwards to induce rainfall.

May: *Vesak* (Buddha Day)

June/July: *Khao Pansa* is the beginning of the Buddhist Lent.

August: *Ho Khao Padap Dinh*, All Saints Day.

Sept/Oct: *Boun ok Pansa* signals the end of the Buddhist Lent.

October: *Boun Lay Heua Phai* is

a colourful water festival with boat races, celebrating the end of the rainy season.

Oct–Nov: the three-day *That Luang* festival centres on the That Luang temple in Vientiane.

Many shops and offices also close for the Chinese and Vietnamese New Year in January or February.

Language

Lao is the official language of Laos. One of the Tai languages of South-East Asia, it's closely related to that spoken in neighbouring Thailand. It's mainly monosyllabic and uses tones to differentiate between words — and fiendishly difficult for Westerners to learn. Luckily, English is widely understood, especially by younger people in urban areas, while French might come in useful with older Laotians.

Media

The bi-weekly *Vientiane Times* offers some insight into the day-to-day life of the nation. See www.vientianetimes.com.

International newspapers other than *The Bangkok Post* are hard to come by, though you might find some old copies of *Asiaweek* and *Time* on sale in bookshops.

Most medium- and top-range hotels have satellite TV, showing channels like CNN and MTV. Short-wave radio enthusiasts can listen to BBC World Service, Voice of America and Radio Australia, but be sure to check the times and frequencies before you leave, as they often change.

Money matters

The unit of currency is the *kip* (KN). The most frequently used notes range from 500 to 100,000 kip. There are no coins currently in circulation. The US dollar is sometimes accepted as cash, and Thai *baht* can be used, especially near the border with Thailand. Many places visited by tourists also accept the Euro.

This is very much a cash economy, although credit cards are taken at many tourist hotels and restaurants in the larger cities. Bring enough money in low denomination US dollar bills to cover such things as meals, travel and shopping for the duration of your holiday. You can obtain cash advances on credit cards at banks and exchange bureaux, but doing so will incur heavy charges. There are ATMs in Vientiane and other large towns.

Make sure you don't change too many dollars or euros into *kip* at any one time: you'll acquire plenty of them in your change anyway, but it isn't a convertible currency; you can change it back at Vientiane airport but banks and exchange bureaux won't buy it back after you've left the country.

Opening Hours

Banks are generally open Monday to Friday, 8.30 a.m. to 4 or 4.30 p.m.

Post offices, as a rule, open Monday to Friday 8 a.m to 5 p.m. and Saturday morning 8 a.m. to noon.

There are no set hours for shops, though they tend to open daily, including Sundays, and keep long hours.

Government offices open from around 8 a.m. to noon and 1 p.m. to 5 p.m.

Temples and monasteries keep more restricted hours, and it's best to get to them in the morning to be sure to find them open.

Photography

Take plenty of memory cards for your digital camera, as well as spare batteries (and your battery charger). Remember that the tropical light is at its best for a couple of hours after sunrise and just before sunset, and very harsh from mid-morning to mid-afternoon. When taking people's photographs, ask for their permission first.

Public Transport

Because of the mountainous terrain and poor roads, travelling overland through Laos is both scenically beautiful and painfully slow. Add to this the rickety nature of the inter-city buses, the uncomfortable seats and the heat, and it can be just painful. The journey time between Vientiane and Luang Prabang, for example, is approximately 10 hours. Still, it's the cheapest way of getting around, and many will argue that it's the best way to see the country—but you will need to spend plenty of time in Laos for this option to be viable.

Given that the country is dominated by the mighty Mekong River and its many tributaries, it's no surprise that the traditional method of transport is by boat. You can travel between the main cities on the Mekong by slow boat (Vientiane-Luang Prabang takes about 5 days) or cruise ships. Less traditional are the incredibly noisy powerboats that cover the distances quickly, but are cramped and uncomfortable.

If you're pressed for time, you'll probably find yourself taking to the air. Lao Airlines is the only airline company operating internal flights in Laos, and flies to most of the larger regional cities. It didn't have the best reputation among the world's airlines but has now upgraded its image and there are some decent newer planes such as the ATR 72 in the fleet.

www.laoairlines.com

In town, the most practical and inexpensive way to get around is by the brightly painted, three-wheel motorcycle taxi known as a Jumbo. This is very much a home-grown product, where a basic carriage is soldered onto a motorbike that has been cut in two. The more famous *tuk-tuk* is the Japanese-made version, popular throughout South-East Asia. The *cyclo*, or cycle-rickshaw, is a slower, but more traditional mode of transport, and rarely sighted these days. There are some taxi cars available, especially at the airports. If you prefer to use one of these at other times, ask your hotel desk to arrange one for you. Whichever type of taxi you take, though, always agree on the price in advance.

Safety
Laos is generally safe for tourists, and its citizens are rarely anything other than friendly and courteous to visitors. But it's also a very poor country, and it's worthwhile taking some basic safety precautions, especially in Vientiane. Make sure valuables are kept in the hotel safe. Carry your passport, cash and travellers cheques in a money belt or sealable pocket, and be especially vigilant in crowded places where pickpockets operate, such as busy tourist sites. Be careful not to stray too far off the beaten track alone at night. If you're heading out into the remoter countryside, check first that the roads are free of bandit activity, and also take extreme caution when walking off main paths: there is still a vast amount of unexploded ordnance left over from the Vietnam War.

Time
Standard time in Laos is UTC/GMT+7.

Tipping
Tipping isn't customary in Laos. But bear in mind that wages are extremely low, and it wouldn't be considered amiss to leave a small tip in hotels and restaurants, at your discretion.

Toilets
Public toilets will be a rare sight on your travels around the country, so whenever you're in tourist-friendly places such as cafés, restaurants, hotels and museums remember to make use of the facilities before leaving.

UNESCO World Heritage Sites
Laos has two sites: the town of Luang Prabang, and Wat Phu and associated settlements within the Champasak cultural landscape.

Voltage
Electric current is generally 220V, 50 cycle AC. Power cuts are not infrequent, although most of the larger hotels now have back-up generators. Bring a torch just in case.

168 INDEX

Airports 162
Baci 156
Ban Saphai 156
Bolaven Plateau 156
Champasak Province 155–157
Climate 162
Communications 162
Dining out 160–161
Driving 163
Emergencies 163
Festivals 164–165
Formalities 163
Health 163–164
History 135–139
Holidays 164–165
Khon Phapheng Falls 157
Kuang Si Waterfall 152
Language 165
Luang Prabang 149–152
 Lower Town 151–152
 Mekong 152
 Night Market 150
 Old City 149–151
 Phu Si 150
 Royal Palace 149–150
 That Pathum 151
 Wat Aham 150
 Wat Chum Khong 150
 Wat Mai 150
 Wat Pakkhan 151
 Wat That 151
 Wat That Luang 151–152
 Wat Visun 150
 Wat Xieng Thong 151
Media 165
Money matters 165–166
Opening Hours 166
Pak Ou Caves 152
Pakse 155–156
Photography 166
Plain of Jars 152–153
Public transport 166–167
Safety 167
Savannakhet 155
Shopping 159
Suan Vathanatham 147
Tham Chang 147
Tham Pha Kam 147
Tham Phum 152
Tham Thing 152
Tham Xang 147
That Ing Hang 155
Time 167
Tipping 167
Toilets 167
Vang Vieng 147
Unesco sites 167
Vientiane 141–147
 City centre 141–145
 Colonial Quarter 143
 Lan Xang Avenue 145
 Lao National Museum 142
 Mekong 144–145
 Nam Phu Place 141
 Patuxai Arch 145
 Pra That Luang 145–147
 Presidential Palace 143
 Talat Sao 145
 Wat Ho Pra Keo 143
 Wat Ong Teu 144
 Wat Si Muang 144
 Wat Si Saket 144
Voltage 167
Wat Chom Phet 152
Wat Long Khun 152
Wat Phu 156–157
Wat Sayaphum 155
Wat Tham 152
Wat Xieng Khuan 147

General editor
Barbara Ender-Jones

Design
Karin Palazzolo

Layout
Luc Malherbe, Matias Jolliet

Photo credits
p. 129: Renata Holzbachová
p. 130: istockphoto.com/
CWLawrence (parasol);
/feoton (temple)
hemis.fr/Body (girl)
fotolia.com/champa (lotus)

Maps
JPM Publications,
Mathieu Germay

Copyright © 2012, 2008
JPM Publications S.A.
12, avenue William-Fraisse,
1006 Lausanne, Suisse
information@jpmguides.com
http://www.jpmguides.com/

All rights reserved. No part of this book may be reproduced or transmitted in any form or by any means, electronic or mechanical, including photocopying, recording or by any information storage and retrieval system without permission in writing from the publisher.

Every care has been taken to verify the information in the guide, but the publisher cannot accept responsibility for any errors that may have occurred. If you spot an inaccuracy or a serious omission, please let us know.

Printed in Germany
15168.00.11023
Edition 2012